"Very helpful, useful and inspiring."

Satish Kumar, *Founder of The Resurgence Trust, Editor Emeritus of Resurgence & Ecologist magazine, Vice-President of RSPCA, Oxfam UK Ambassador and Author of countless articles and books including* No Destination

"Reading *Leading Beyond Sustainability* has inspired me to contribute to making our collective future as bright as possible. It has helped me make more sense of our world, relate deeply to the challenges we face, and has given me more courage to do something about them. On reflection, I can do much more. I've taken a personal vow to collaborate, to lead, and to act 'beyond sustainability'. I very much appreciate this book. Thank you, Clive."

Neill Morley, *Senior Business Engagement Manager, DLA Piper*

"Whether you think you can make a difference for a more sustainable world or not, this book is for you!"

Amcara, *Consultants in Consciousness Evolution for a Sustainable World*

"Clive Wilson's book *Leading Beyond Sustainability* is an essential read for people searching for universal wellbeing. By following his unique perspective of six aspirations – Peace, Connection, Abundance, Vitality, Wisdom and Opportunity, people can have a brighter future and live in a better world. In his aspiration for peace, which he defines as no war and declining violence, he introduces a radical idea, Establishing Departments / Ministries for Peace in every government of the world, an idea which he got from my book *How Not to Go to War*. This idea has the potential of building a peaceful world by proactive actions to stop the potential conflicts before they start. *Leading Beyond Sustainability* is a ground-breaking book which has the potential of building a safe, equitable and sustainable world."

Vijay Mehta, *Author of* How Not to Go to War *and Chair Uniting for Peace; Founding Trustee, Fortune Forum Charity; Board Member, GAMIP (Global Alliance for Ministries and Infrastructures for Peace)*

"Clive's book is a massive undertaking encouraging us to engage in securing a brighter future. The book's scope is broad covering what Clive calls his six aspirations, or you could call them pillars, that frame the undertaking of creating a brighter future. The aspirations of connection, peace, vitality, abundance, opportunity and wisdom create a vast compelling picture to guide us. His narrative is enlivened by the stories of people he has met or worked with and each chapter ends with an invitation to research, reflect and decide your own actions towards a brighter future. The book is also about leadership beyond sustainability and Clive's leadership framework, also illuminated with stories, is easy to follow and linked to his aspirations. Because the book is also an invitation to notice, encourage and celebrate actions that are moving us towards a better future, I recommend reading the book twice (at least!): The first time to embrace the hypothesis and stories and the second to follow Clive's encouragement to research stuff for yourself and also to connect with your own life story."

John Campbell, *Founder of Primeast*

"Clive is a true advocate of leadership and has held a life-long career supporting leaders to create a vision in which purpose sets the foundations for delivering success. In his latest book, he brings to the forefront innovative thought-provoking concepts which take 'Leadership Beyond Sustainability', inspiring those who recognise that leading means much more than just economic success. Good leadership contributes positively to the world in which we live and supports our global environment, now and for the future. Clive presents real-life examples to demonstrate ways in which high-performing teams are aligned to the world in which we all live.

Once again, Clive has produced an insightful and interesting read for anyone looking to develop their knowledge of leadership and I highly recommend it to those who aspire to shape a sustainable future for their business and for future generations."

Tim Hopkinson, *Director, E. Poppleton & Son Ltd, Wales*

"This is a beautiful, thought-provoking book, full of gently challenging questions and inspiring stories of people who possess a willingness to believe that we can all, in our own small and unique ways, change the world. It is a book about the power of noticing and the power of gratitude. In this work, Clive has also provided us with a workbook to help us with our reflective practice and space and time to think about how we are going about our work in relation to ourselves, those that we love, those who we work with, and our relationship with the world. I don't know anyone else who could have written this book. It is a testament to Clive's energetic, unapologetic and enthusiastic optimism, and to our shared belief in the possibility of something better."

Matt Walsh, *Consultant and past Chief Officer in UK National Health Service*

"Holding the tension between the beauty and sometimes brutality of life, Clive Wilson, in *Leading Beyond Sustainability*, boldly envisions with examples from around the world how we all, as leaders, can build on those that have gone before us to go beyond sustainability and reach that brighter future for all."

Chris Burford, *Turnaround Director and Psychotherapist*

"This important book is what our world needs at this point in time when we are constantly bombarded with negative news and disparity. Clive is generously providing lots of convincing sources of data, cases, own experiences, constructive ideas and reflective questions which are both encouraging and inspiring guidance for how you can act and contribute to a more sustainable life for all on this earth!"

Tor Eneroth, *Founder, Amcara*

"Reading Clive's book is like sitting by a warm fireside with a mug of (sustainably sourced) cocoa, while a kindly wisdom keeper shares his knowledge, experience, passion and encouragement so that we, the readers, can move to deeper levels of being. From that space, we can be inspired to join the global movement that is already transforming life on earth."

Phil Clothier, *Founder, Amcara*

"This book is truly wonderful with so many different voices testifying to a future that is very much in play."

Francesca Walker-Martin, *Reader in Work Based Learning, Degree Apprenticeship Lead at the University of Central Lancashire, CMI Approved Centre Director and ASET Chair*

Leading Beyond Sustainability

The 2020s present a decade of unprecedented disruption. We have now reached a point where people are overwhelmed and numb to the ever-present news of threat after threat, and challenge after challenge. It's time for leaders to tell a different story of six powerful aspirations – connection, vitality, peace, abundance, opportunity and wisdom. This is a vision "beyond sustainability", to inspire organisations and people to bring the best of who they are into service of the brighter future that is already emerging.

Alongside the obvious disruptive challenges of climate change, wars and the pandemic, technology has evolved at a blistering pace. Through technological advances in five sectors – energy, transport, materials, food and manufacturing – we are already transforming the world as we know it. The book seeks to give readers the confidence that there is real hope for a brighter future for our world using these developments and other innovations.

The text is supported by inspiring case studies of people and organisations who are already doing amazing things. Crucially, the book highlights the many ways that leaders and organisations can contribute to a better world and encourages dialogue between organisations and people who might not naturally connect. It describes 12 archetypes in organisations that must collaborate in teams to deliver solutions. It also emphasises the need for wise leadership and conscious alignment of everyone to our "brighter future".

A manifesto for positive change, this is the perfect book to help turn the UN Sustainable Development Goals into action and to envisage a positive future for leaders at every level in organisations.

Clive Wilson is an author, speaker, facilitator and leadership coach who has specialised in "purposeful leadership" for over 20 years. He has two previously published books: *Designing the Purposeful Organization* and *Designing the Purposeful World*. His passion is to help leaders consciously create the conditions for a brighter future. He has worked extensively across all continents and with many household-name businesses.

Leading Beyond Sustainability

Six Aspirations for a Brighter Future

CLIVE WILSON

LONDON AND NEW YORK

Designed cover image: Clive Wilson

First published 2025
by Routledge
4 Park Square, Milton Park, Abingdon, Oxon OX14 4RN

and by Routledge
605 Third Avenue, New York, NY 10158

Routledge is an imprint of the Taylor & Francis Group, an informa business

© 2025 Clive Wilson

The right of Clive Wilson to be identified as author of this work has been asserted in accordance with sections 77 and 78 of the Copyright, Designs and Patents Act 1988.

All rights reserved. No part of this book may be reprinted or reproduced or utilised in any form or by any electronic, mechanical, or other means, now known or hereafter invented, including photocopying and recording, or in any information storage or retrieval system, without permission in writing from the publishers.

Trademark notice: Product or corporate names may be trademarks or registered trademarks, and are used only for identification and explanation without intent to infringe.

British Library Cataloguing-in-Publication Data
A catalogue record for this book is available from the British Library

Library of Congress Cataloging-in-Publication Data
Names: Wilson, Clive, 1955– author.
Title: Leading beyond sustainability : six aspirations for a brighter future / Clive Wilson.
Description: Abingdon, Oxon ; New York, NY : Routledge, 2025. |
Includes bibliographical references and index.
Identifiers: LCCN 2024014362 | ISBN 9781032549248 (hardback) |
ISBN 9781032549255 (paperback) | ISBN 9781003428121 (ebook)
Subjects: LCSH: Management–Environmental aspects. |
Sustainable development. | Leadership.
Classification: LCC HD30.255 .W549 2025 |
DDC 658.4/083–dc23/eng/20240614
LC record available at https://lccn.loc.gov/2024014362

Every effort has been made to contact copyright-holders. Please advise the publisher of any errors or omissions, and these will be corrected in subsequent editions.

ISBN: 978-1-032-54924-8 (hbk)
ISBN: 978-1-032-54925-5 (pbk)
ISBN: 978-1-003-42812-1 (ebk)

DOI: 10.4324/9781003428121

Typeset in Dante and Avenir
by Newgen Publishing UK

Contents

Foreword by Heath Jackson — xi

Introduction: Why "beyond" sustainability? — 1

PART I What is *beyond* sustainability? The six aspirations — **11**

1 The power of connection — 13

2 The freedom of peace — 37

3 The joy of vitality — 60

4 A spirit of abundance — 83

5 Infinite opportunity — 105

6 Profound wisdom — 116

PART II Leading a diverse team of players — **131**

7 A role for everyone: Twelve archetypes — 133

8 Who are you and how do you relate to others? — 143

x Contents

9 Leading the action 151

PART III The Wisdom Code: Why mankind needs a new approach to personal, corporate and global leadership 159

10 Why wisdom and why now? 161

11 The Wisdom Code 171

PART IV Global alignment 179

12 Total and conscious alignment to a brighter future 181

Index 199

Foreword

Heath Jackson

I first worked with Clive back in 2019 – in a time we now widely refer to as pre-pandemic. I specifically mention that as the global pandemic of 2020 has fundamentally changed the way we think about work, relationships and our general approach to living our lives. At that time, Clive was working with me and my Leadership Team colleagues at KPMG on how we engaged our people in our purpose, why we wanted to work in the firm and what we all wanted to get out of that experience. Looking back, we were right in the Zeitgeist as that sense of purpose is featuring larger and larger in how we think about our work and home lives, how we balance them and how we get a more positive outcome in both. Clive covers this in his 2018 book *Designing the Purposeful World*.

My work with Clive at that time not only changed how I engaged with my teams in KPMG but also set in train a major thought process for me personally – one that would fundamentally change my work life and lead me to doing the things I now get so much fulfilment from. Based on those early discussions and to a degree by the pandemic and the inevitable changes to the ways we worked, in 2020, I started on the process of planning my retirement from KPMG and what I might want to do in the future. I was involved in the construction of the Nightingale Hospital in the Harrogate Convention Centre in the early frightening days of 2020 – we can argue about the need and use of that exercise but what I did learn is how much people can achieve in a very short space of time by working towards a common goal. Everyone pulling in the same direction with a clear plan creates something I have never seen before in my career – truly inspiring human behaviour.

xii Foreword

I have been interested in renewable energy and conservation for many years. My wife and I had rebuilt an old Yorkshire farmhouse over a two-year period starting in 2016, with the idea of creating a "new house" within an old one – big focus on insulation and efficient heating with a ground source heat pump through to installation of the largest domestic solar panel array possible complete with batteries. This led to further thoughts on how we might use the land we own to have a positive effect on the environment through mitigation of man-made climate change from the effects of CO_2 and create a better natural environment for wildlife.

Clive and I continued to chat. My career had changed from that of a senior partner at KPMG to an adviser for a number of fast-growing technology firms but only those firms with a clear purpose and a desire to make the world a better place. One of those roles has introduced me to Callum Fitzgerald, a technology entrepreneur but a marine biologist by background. Callum told me all about Ecopia Marine[1] and the plans to create "climostats" to enable the control of the man-made CO_2 in the atmosphere by harnessing the power of the Oceans and the smallest life forms within them. The capture of light at the surface of the ocean and distributing it to the nutrient-rich but dark depths lead to an explosion of plankton and the subsequent sequestration of carbon. A brighter future in many definitions and certainly one I am enjoying in helping make a reality.

So why read Clive's latest book? For me, leadership is everything, and often what leaders lack is an understanding of the very next step they should take and positively utilise the shadow they cast by their position. How do we learn as leaders to look to the future and take those next steps? Clive's engineering background lays out logical steps we can follow. A book you can read cover to cover or dip in as needed to give you insights on how you can form your own "what's next". I guarantee one thing – the brighter future is out there – you just need the steps to get there.

Note

1 Ecopia, 2024. www.ecopia.world

Introduction

Why "beyond" sustainability?

When the karate master seeks to smash the plank of wood or block of stone, they know to aim beyond the obstacle. Their target is not the obstacle. It is the place beyond it.

For many of us, the same is true of sustainability. I deliberately use the word "many" because there are millions of people doing amazing work to avoid devastation from the ills that challenge our precious world. They wish to see an end to poverty, hunger, poor education, runaway climate change, destruction of habitat, war, injustice and much more. I totally and utterly celebrate their essential work in the world.

Indeed, when world leaders signed onto the United Nations Sustainable Development Goals[1] (SDGs) in 2015, I celebrated with many others. Here, for the first time in the history of humankind was a vision we could all buy into. A world free from the scourges described above. I was inspired and evolved my career plan to devote time to play my part. I wrote *Designing the Purposeful World – the Sustainable Development Goals as a Blueprint for Humanity* (Routledge 2018)[2] as a sequel to *Designing the Purposeful Organisation – How to Inspire Business Performance Beyond Boundaries* (Kogan Page 2015).[3] I established the Harrogate branch of the United Nations Association to encourage local action, and I set up a Facebook page for the SDGs which achieved over 30,000 followers before it closed in 2023.

I also began to speak wherever I could to engage audiences in the SDGs. I consider myself fortunate to have worked in this way with

DOI: 10.4324/9781003428121-1

2 Introduction

thousands of people from the age of seven to well over 70 across three continents. I typically began by asking them to close their eyes and visit anywhere in the world they would like to go. These explorers have (in their mind's eye) visited cities, forests, oceans – indeed every corner of our precious world.

I am always inspired when audiences share their adventures with each other, but two of their stories hold a very special place in my heart.

Cleaning up the oceans

A young man visited a place deep in the ocean and commented how beautiful it was – teaming with life and free from plastic and other debris. This was a stark contrast to his experiences as a scuba diver. He commented that this journey inspired him to devote his career to cleaning up the oceans.

Children were laughing, parents enjoyed coffee and the buildings were beautiful

A 10-year-old girl visited a playground in Syria. The children were smiling, laughing and playing, whilst their parents sat in cafes in the street opposite enjoying coffee and some working on their laptops – and the buildings were beautiful!

A powerful vision of six aspirations

To me, these are visions of a world "beyond sustainability". They are visions of a fabulous, gorgeous world that we will be delighted to live in. They are visions of paradise. This world inspires me.

Recently, I challenged myself to summarise this paradise under six headings. Why six? Because even after working intimately with the 17 SDGs, I still struggle to list them all and remember their numbers. So here are my "six aspirations". I would really love to know how they resonate with you (Figure 0.1).

I've also done an analysis of these six to see how they encompass the essence of the SDGs. Here is my analysis. It's not an exact science (Figure 0.2).

Introduction 3

Figure 0.1 Six aspirations for a brighter future.

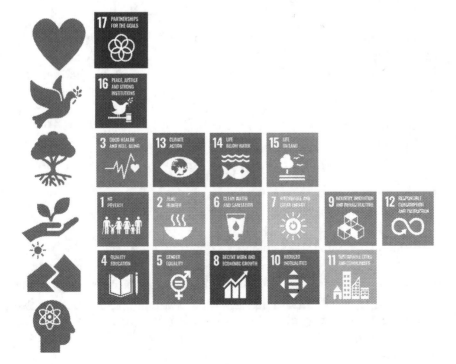

Figure 0.2 Comparing the six aspirations to the 17 UN Sustainable Development Goals.

4 Introduction

Wisdom is key

One thing I noticed after my analysis is that "Wisdom" stands out as one to which I didn't attribute any single SDG. I guess we could argue that all 17 of the goals require wisdom but I've left it as a new part of my "beyond sustainability" vision as a vital ingredient worthy of special attention. It is for this reason that Part III of this book is dedicated to this subject, including an opportunity to use a simple diagnostic to identify ways each one of us can actively develop and nurture our own wisdom. This Wisdom Code is in Chapter 9 of this book.

Another thing that really inspires me is the fact that there are so many millions of individuals and organisations working towards one or more of my set of six aspirations. If you are (or represent) one of them, please let me know. I would like to celebrate your work. Just contact me on LinkedIn so we can discuss the best way to do this.

Hope and confidence

I want to explain the reason for my hope and confidence that we will deliver the paradise we all dream of. My reason relates to my understanding of the way purpose works. This understanding can be summarised in three powerful principles:

1. Life in a context
2. Self-similarity
3. The observer

1. Life in a context

The "life in a context" principle was significantly inspired by the work of Dr Bruce Lipton who discovered that tissue grown from human stem cells would take one form (such as heart tissue) if the stem cell is placed in one solution and a different form (perhaps lung tissue) if it is placed in another. This insight is not only invaluable for the science of organ transplants, but it also suggests that life-purpose is an energetic reaction between a life form and its environment.

2. Self-similarity

The second principle is "self-similarity", inspired by the work of Benoit Mandelbrot,[4] the "father of fractal mathematics". He noticed repeating patterns of self-similarity throughout the natural world. This can be seen in clouds, coastlines, ferns and countless other places. This helps us to understand that purpose arises when life at any scale is placed in a context. So, what works for stem cells is equally true of humans, teams, organisations and all of humanity.

3. The observer

Thirdly, the "observer" principle suggests that purpose depends on who is looking at a situation. To put it another way, it is how the life form experiences itself and its context. This is a vital component of Purposeful Leadership which, when understood, can help leaders maximise the power of purpose to deliver change – which is what leaders do.

Humanity has the potential to deliver a better world

The way these three powerful principles play out in *Leading Beyond Sustainability* is remarkable. I suggest that it is reasonable to assume that there is huge diversity and capability in humanity. I got a glimpse of this recently when I was returning to consciousness after an operation. I rested quietly in my hospital bed and marvelled at the diversity of talent that made my operation successful. Not just the surgeon, but the anaesthetist, the nurses, the catering staff, the engineers who built the hospital, the pharmacists – and this is just the tip of the iceberg. In fact, later in this book as we examine people who are working to deliver Vitality, I celebrate the work of Poppleton, a company in beautiful North Wales, which makes ventilation systems, many of which end up in hospitals and are critical to their functioning.

I suggest that this plays out for every challenge, known and unknown, to humanity. People are working to solve problems, deliver solutions and collaborate with others to make the system work. And if they're not doing so now, someone somewhere is being sufficiently curious and innovative

6 Introduction

to do so when the time is right. This all stems from the three principles described above. Everyone (to a greater or lesser extent) has a capability the world needs. Their purpose is being stimulated by something going on in the world that they feel drawn to.

Optimism or rationalism?

For many people, the prospect of an evolving *brighter future* is overly *optimistic*. Indeed, I would have categorised myself as an optimist until I discovered the work of Canadian-American cognitive psychologist Steven Pinker. Pinker is the Johnstone Family Professor at Harvard University and author of several books, many of which are relevant to my thinking here in *Leading Beyond Sustainability*.

I particularly appreciate Pinker's thinking behind his 2021 book on *Rationality* where he affirms that he is not an optimist. Rather he is a *rationalist* and bases his conclusion, that life for humanity is improving in many ways, on robust research and data.

This book is presented in the same vein as Pinker's thinking. It encourages you to check out the latest evidence, explore the data, read case studies, hear some of my personal encounters and contemplate your own – all to support the notion that there has never been a better time (for most of us) to be alive. As I've been writing this book, I have scoured the Internet for data to evidence the case that our "brighter future" is indeed emerging and rapidly. At first, I began to pepper the text with this evidence but realised that data soon becomes out of date and superseded. So, in the first six chapters, I have included activities for you as a reader to check out data for yourself. In most cases, I will point you to the "Our World in Data" website.[5] Why have I chosen this resource over and above the plethora of others? Well, I hope this extract from the "about" page on the site explains my reasoning:

> Poverty, disease, hunger, climate change, war, existential risks, and inequality: The world faces many great and terrifying problems. It is these large problems that our work at Our World in Data focuses on.
>
> Thanks to the work of thousands of researchers around the world who dedicate their lives to it, we often have a good understanding of how it is possible to make progress against the large problems we are facing. The world has the resources to do much better and reduce the suffering in the world.

Introduction **7**

We believe that a key reason why we fail to achieve the progress we are capable of is that we do not make enough use of this existing research and data: the important knowledge is often stored in inaccessible databases, locked away behind paywalls and buried under jargon in academic papers.

The goal of our work is to make the knowledge on the big problems accessible and understandable. As we say on our homepage, Our World in Data's mission is to publish the "research and data to make progress against the world's largest problems".

Of course, there is no guarantee that this valuable resource will always be available. However, please note that it is produced as a collaborative effort between researchers at the University of Oxford, who are the scientific contributors of the website content, and the non-profit organisation Global Change Data Lab that owns, publishes and maintains the website and the data tools.

In the unlikely event that this resource becomes unavailable, please simply check out other sources. I trust you will find that, despite the many backward steps, humanity is indeed progressing rapidly to a brighter future.

Self-organising complexity

The mathematics of supply and demand also works to help us self-organise our contributions. If we see that some purposes are over-subscribed but others are under-subscribed, we may develop a sense of urgency to go where we are needed or *called* – providing we are the right person with the right skills for the job. We see this work at parties. The musician sits at the piano. Someone else starts to sing. The chef cooks a delicious meal. The social angel notices the person at a loose-end and talks to them. Someone fills the empty glasses and we all have a good time.

Yes, this sounds like the best of parties, and we know it isn't always like that. But it works well enough for most of us to enjoy most parties, most of the time! So it is with the creation of our paradise.

Even if we don't fill the *technical* roles of creating our paradise, there are so many other roles we can and do fill. We may think that what we need in the world is a bunch of scientists and engineers innovating our way through and beyond the challenges we face. Well, yes we do – but we also need people to inspire them, to encourage them and to build enterprises around them. One of my favourite personal thoughts is this:

8 Introduction

Every time we notice, encourage and celebrate someone who is changing the world, we are changing the world.

I frequently post these words on my LinkedIn profile banner and use them in my presentations at conference.

Think about it. Who do you know that is doing an amazing job – making the world a better place? If you've noticed them, what have you done to encourage and celebrate their achievements?

The innovator and the encourager are just 2 of 12 archetypal roles that I describe in Part II of this book. These are (in my humble opinion) some of the key personalities that come together to make paradise a reality. By the way, only nine of these characters are positive. There are a couple of renegades in the mix and one who simply isn't playing. But life's like that.

This is more than a book – make sure you keep a journal or learning log

Throughout this book, I will ask you to pause from reading for a few minutes and do something. It may be to check out data on trends and other statistics online. It may be to reflect on who you know that is changing the world. It might be to ask you to acknowledge them and celebrate their work. For this reason, right from the outset, I encourage you to dedicate a notebook to use as a journal or learning log. This will be an invaluable resource to help you make the most of this book. I also hope you'll find a way to share your most profound insights with others to inspire them to join us in our journey to a brighter future.

The power of poetry

For many years, I have been moved to write poetry. It is something that, until recently, I have kept aside from my professional career in Purposeful Leadership. However, in recent years, I have been encouraged, by friends and associates, especially Matt Walsh, Phil Clothier and Tor Eneroth (who you will meet later) to weave my poetry into my work. I can't begin to tell you how much courage it initially took to recite my poems at conferences and even at funerals (including my Dad's). Matt kindly encouraged me to share poetry with him (he's an amazing poet) and audiences and to engage with them and ask what meaning they gained from the experience. Matt and

Introduction **9**

I were inspired to hear that the listener (or reader) often gleaned wisdom that the poet hadn't intended. It's as if the poet is simply a vehicle for something unique and powerful for each receiver.

This is my way of gently seeking your permission to share some of my poetry in this book. I hope it adds a different dimension to the plain text, bringing the intended thinking to life and inspiring your leadership in some small way.

Notes

1 United Nations, 2024. UN SDGs: https://sdgs.un.org/goals
2 Wilson, C. A. 2018. "Designing the Purposeful World": www.routledge.com/ Designing-the-Purposeful-World-The-Sustainable-Development-Goals-as-a-Blueprint/Wilson/p/book/9780815381327
3 Wilson, C. A. 2015. "Designing the Purposeful Organization": www.koganp age.com/hr-learning-development/designing-the-purposeful-organization-9780749472207
4 Wikipedia, 2024. Benoit Mandelbrot: https://en.wikipedia.org/wiki/Benoit_Mandelbrot
5 Our World in Data, 2024. Our World in Data: https://ourworldindata.org/

Part I

What is *beyond* sustainability?

The six aspirations

In this part of *Leading Beyond Sustainability*, we examine the six aspirations chapter by chapter to offer a compelling narrative for each and case studies or "personal encounters" demonstrating how each aspiration is in motion. I make no apology for the fact that these "encounters" are from my own experience. This serves multiple purposes:

1. These encounters are intended to showcase and provide inspiration for how anyone can take steps to make a difference (especially within organisations and the world of work).
2. I use examples that I'm personally connected to because I can speak first-hand.
3. It will almost certainly be the case that you, the reader, will know of other examples from your personal experience.
4. Encouraging you to begin thinking like this will hopefully inspire you to notice, encourage and celebrate people in your own life who are changing the world.
5. It also reminds us that the world changes through the millions of (seemingly relatively small) actions taken each day by millions of people – arguably just as much as it does through the fewer major breakthroughs and disruptions that make the news headlines.
6. This is a deliberate strategy to make the point that we all know of work that is happening on many fronts to deliver the future world we want to see.
7. The sum total of all this work is enormous and probably far, far greater than anyone could reasonably account for.

DOI: 10.4324/9781003428121-2

12 What is *beyond* sustainability? The six aspirations

This is no pipe dream. This is a world that is emerging and one to which leaders can and do choose to consciously align.

Taking hope and gaining confidence from the power of personal action is not to suggest that humanity should not strive to measure and account for gains made in a positive direction, especially where action is significant and in mitigation of known threats. Nor does it detract from the responsibility of any organisation of any type, especially governments to account for their delivery against manifestos and declared strategies. Nor should it detract from the duty of each one of us to do the right thing, with our "brighter future" as our true north.

The personal encounters I have used may not be the most significant ones to demonstrate positive momentum. But the power of personal connection is massively important. It is in such circumstances that I am best able to notice, encourage and celebrate people and organisations who are changing the world. My encouragement to you, the reader, is to do the same.

Many of my personal encounters are further brought to life on my YouTube channel.[1] Here you will find videos of many conversations I've had with those featured in my personal encounters. These and other references are also held in an article[2] on my LinkedIn page.[3] Visiting these sources makes accessing additional resources easy for you, the reader, by having clickable links. You can, of course, also contact me directly to find out more.

Chapter by chapter, I encourage you to make a note of your own personal encounters (notice). I encourage you to share such enterprise on LinkedIn or other social media (celebrate) and copy those involved with your personal words of encouragement (encourage).

Forgive me for repeating these vital words:

Every time we notice, encourage and celebrate people who are changing the world, we are changing the world.

Notes

1   Wilson, C. A. 2024. Author's YouTube channel: www.youtube.com/cliveawilson
2   Wilson, C. A. 2024. Article on author's LinkedIn page: www.linkedin.com/pulse/leading-beyond-sustainability-six-aspirations-brighter-clive-wilson-nclte
3   Wilson, C. A. 2024. Author's LinkedIn page: www.linkedin.com/in/cliveawilson/

The power of connection   1

Connection

> How blessed are we
> To live in a world
> Where a thought becomes a word
> And a word is shared in an instant
> With those who might need it
>
> How blessed are we to know
> What's happening anywhere
> That we might care
> To share their joy
> Or feel their pain
> And plan our days
> In helpful ways
>
> How blessed to know
> Love stretches
> All around the world and beyond
> That far from alone
> We share this amazing journey
> With all of life
>
> When we close our eyes
> And pause
> We can soar with the birds

DOI: 10.4324/9781003428121-3

14 What is *beyond* sustainability? The six aspirations

> Run with the deer
> Breathe with the forest
> Dive in the oceans
> Swim with the fish
> And strange creatures
> We've never seen before
>
> We can stand beside soldiers
> In the trenches
> And with their mums
> And their children
> We can shed tears at the thought
> And act if we ought
>
> We can sit with the dying
> Hold their hands
> And gaze into their eyes
> Sharing the start
> Of a new journey for their heart
>
> How blessed are we?[1]

Humanity is technically more connected than ever and advancing rapidly. We are also realising how much more emotionally connected we need to be and how much we must take account of our ecological connection with all of life on our planet.

When I began thinking about the six aspirations, the one I finally decided to name "connection" could very easily have been labelled "love", but I opted for "connection" as a term that embraces the use of technical systems to support our exchange of knowledge and ideas and to simply meet and engage with other people, as well as the vital need to be connected emotionally, with compassion, love and kindness – to each other, to all of life and to this gorgeous planet we call "home". Indeed, a crucial and emerging insight is that we are all one. This concept of "unity consciousness" has been recognised and taught by wisdom traditions for thousands of years and is now beginning to be substantiated by the work of quantum physicists. Bob Anderson has more to say about this in Chapter 6 when we discuss the subject of wisdom.

The power of connection **15**

> ## ACTIVITY
>
> As mentioned in my introduction, I invite you to check out the most recent data to show how our interconnection has progressed and continues to progress. Visit the Our World in Data website and explore the evidence of trends that are available there. Pay particular attention to any data that relates to the way we connect with each other. This might include technological changes such as the growth of Internet, social media and artificial intelligence. But also take a look at less obvious topics such as the growth in tourism and democracy, both of which serve to connect people to each other and perhaps some of the environmental topics that reflect how we are connected to wider ecosystems. Make a note in your journal of your consequential thoughts and conclusions.

Unprecedented technical connection

We are at a critical stage in our evolution where our technical ability to connect is advancing at a lightning pace. It's hard to believe that computer scientist Tim Berners-Lee released the source code for the first web browser and editor as recently as 30 April 1993. Five years later, in 1998, Larry Page and Sergey Brin officially launched Google to market what has become the world's most-used web-based search engine.[2] Since then, it seems that most of our life has gone "online".

In 2020, during the Covid-19 global pandemic, the pace was particularly accelerated. Online working became the default for about half the UK population. In 2023, remote, online or hybrid working continues to be an increasing trend which I suspect will continue to grow, especially as robotics and artificial intelligence (AI) disrupt the workplace.

Speaking of which, in the 2020s we are now experiencing a step change in our ability to connect and process knowledge as AI makes its way into our lives. The Internet and search engines gave us instant access to knowledge, but AI now enables us not only to access information but also to process it, not just as words but also as audio, video, mathematics and in ways that integrate to any imaginable process, from medicine, through transport, energy and manufacturing right through to food production and even government.

16 What is *beyond* sustainability? The six aspirations

In praise of supply chains

Throughout this book, I have tried to put some unlikely or unexpected case studies in to my "personal encounters". Stories include companies likes Poppleton, which manufactures and installs air movement systems for hospitals and pharmaceutical laboratories; Farragut, which develops software for inland revenue collection on behalf of American authorities; and Axia Digital, also in the software space, which makes it possible for nurses to move quickly and easily to support the demands of the UK National Health Service. These are just a few examples of the many organisations who operate as part of the complex and diverse supply chains that keep the wheels of industry and services going.

Many of these suppliers are so focused on their specialisms that they forget and certainly don't take credit for the essential parts they play in making our world a better place. The truth is that every player in a supply chain matters enormously, and we should celebrate their efforts, without which our brighter future would simply not happen.

"A horse! A horse! My kingdom for a horse"

All this reminds me of the well-known story of the fight between King Richard III and his enemy Henry. My abridged version is as follows:

Before the battle, the King's horse needed new shoes. The blacksmith made the shoes and fitted two of them, only to discover that he didn't have enough nails to properly fit the remaining two. The groom was in a hurry to get the horse to the King so asked the blacksmith to use what nails he had as best as he could – rather than take time to make all the ones needed for a proper job.

The battle raged. King Richard rode around, cheering his men and fighting his foes. His enemy, Henry, who wished to be King, was pressing hard.

On the other side of the field, King Richard saw his men falling back. So, he spurred his horse to ride to their aid.

Halfway across the stony field, one of the horse's shoes flew off. The horse was lamed on a rock. Then another shoe came off. The horse stumbled, and the King was thrown heavily to the ground.

Before the King could rise, his frightened horse, although lame, had galloped away. The King looked and saw that his soldiers were beaten and that the battle was going against him. He waved his sword in the air and famously shouted, "A horse! A horse! My kingdom for a horse". But there was no horse for him. His soldiers were intent on saving themselves.

The battle was lost. King Richard was lost. Henry became King of England "all for the want of a horseshoe nail"[3]:

> For the want of a nail the shoe was lost,
> For the want of a shoe the horse was lost,
> For the want of a horse the battle was lost,
> For the failure of battle the kingdom was lost,
> And all for the want of a horseshoe nail.

Supply chains powered by technology

Today, we have a sophisticated web of supply chains, often powered by the most sophisticated technology, coupled with transport and financial systems. Whatever the component or service, we can simply go online, find it, order it, have it delivered (if required) and pay for it. All this connectivity should give us hope and confidence in humanity to make things happen.

The need for balance

When I was a programme manager in the electricity industry, I learnt an important lesson. It's all very well getting the technical aspects of change, as suggested above, sorted out. We also need to balance this with the emotional and behavioural aspects. Indeed, most commentators seem to agree that AI, in particular, needs to be introduced and evolved sensitively with wisdom and ethical consideration.

This is where compassion, love and kindness come into play. There is no doubt that people struggle with change. Lives are turned upside down, jobs are lost, whole populations are forced to migrate and other forms of life on our planet suffer in the process. These factors are calling us to up our game. The technical side of connection should, if we manage it well, give us more time. If AI, call-centre bots and robotic manufacturing are doing a high proportion of our work, it should, in theory, free up time. This is time humanity can invest in, must invest in, caring for each other and our world.

As Jimi Hendrix, so powerfully affirmed, "When the power of love overcomes the love of power, the world will know peace".[4]

18 What is *beyond* sustainability? The six aspirations

When I began my working life as a student engineer with the Yorkshire Electricity Board in 1972 and indeed throughout my time in the electricity industry until 1999, the word "love" was rarely spoken in the workplace.

Despite growing up as teenagers in the 1960s when "love" was fashionably spoken about and sung about as an antidote to violence and war, I don't think my "hippy" generation quite knew how all-pervasive the power of love was, is and always will be.

Have you ever looked up the definition of love in the dictionary? It's quite an education. We can read about romantic love, the act of making love, loving people, groups of people, animals, things and activities.

However, our understanding of love has evolved with our understanding of science. In "Leading a Purposeful Life",[5] I speak of love as the creative power of the universe:

> I hope by now, you will be happy to accept that we are consciousness in flow, love in action. Our true nature is intelligent energy manifesting in the material world. Our energy is one with the energy of everything that is, flowing freely in the co-creation of the universe, guided by our experience of the world around us and beyond us.

Indeed, most of the world's religions suggest that "God is love". In other words, and even to the non-religious, the thing that is behind all of creation is love. It is the greatest connecting force of all and even lies behind all other types of connection and evolution. Think about how we speak of:

- Love for each other
- Love for friends and family
- Love of our communities
- Love of our homes
- Love of our hometown
- Love of adventure
- Love of art
- Love of work and service
- Love of life
- Love for humanity
- Love of our planet

And especially, in the context of this book, we speak of love of a "brighter future" – a future beyond sustainability – a future that embraces all the loves suggested above and a hundred or more other loves.

Figure 1.1 Movement away from fear or towards love.

As a practitioner in Purposeful Leadership, from time to time, I talk about motivation. When doing so, I naturally find myself drawing the three shapes in Figure 1.1 on a whiteboard or flipchart. I explain that the explosion depicts fear, the heart depicts something we love and the arrow depicts our action (or movement), either away from fear or towards love.

I guess that's why I'm writing this book. Whilst fear is a great motivator (who wouldn't run away from a burning building?), most of us are more inspired by a brighter future and certainly experience the process in a better way. The adventure to a "brighter future" is, I believe, the greatest adventure known to humanity.

Compassion

I like to think of compassion as a particular form of love that is felt in response to the challenge or pain felt by a life form. The life form could be another person, a community, an animal or plant, a species, an ecosystem or the whole of our living planet. Equally, it could be me or a part of me.

Compassion is a subset of love. It is part of love, and there is love beyond and separate from compassion. It is fair to say, in sequence, the following:

We (and all of life) are "in love".
Because of this inescapable fact, I sense your pain and feel compassion.
Because we are "in love", I am moved to respond with kindness.

So, love, compassion and kindness are all part of the same creative power. They work as one connecting system, continually evolving the universe.

20 What is *beyond* sustainability? The six aspirations

Kindness

So, kindness is a response (in love) to our compassion for life. Herein lies a serious challenge. Going back to our highly (technically) connected world, we know and can come to know vast amounts of information regarding the suffering of life on our planet. Is there any wonder that many of us feel overwhelmed, anxious, depressed or helpless? In years gone by, if a war broke out on the other side of the world, we may not even hear about it. Today, we not only hear it, we see it. We see the grieving mothers of soldiers sent as cannon fodder to the front line. We see injured, orphaned or starving children with tears in their eyes. We see once-beautiful cities reduced to rubble. We see forests on fire and people and animals fleeing for their lives. The two extreme responses are hearts that break or become numb to the pain.

We feel compassion personally, but we know we cannot solve all the problems of the world. We simply don't have enough kindness in our kitbag. This is where we should take hope from our connected world. This is why connection is one of only six aspirations for a better world articulated in this book.

As Stephen Stills reminded us in song with Crosby, Stills and Nash in 1970, "Love the one you're with"[6]. In other words, we act with kindness as the world is presented to us, moment by moment, during our lives. If we meet everyone we pass with a smile, help those who need our help and encourage those who we notice striving for a brighter future, we will be contributing far more than we know. If, on top of that, we (a) take stock of our own talents and resources and (b) contemplate what it is we most care about, then (in the words of Laurence Boldt – "Zen and the Art of Making a Living"[7]) what excuse will we have not to point (a) at (b) – *with kindness?*

Great connectors – Greta Thunberg and David Attenborough

If you had to think of two famous people who most vividly represented the power of connection for environmental matters in the world today, I wonder who they would be. I can think of several but the two most well-known on my list would be Greta Thunberg and David Attenborough. I especially like the way their methods of connection are so different. In Part II of this book, I describe 12 archetypes that influence the delivery of our brighter future. Feel free to turn briefly to the diagram at the start of Part II to see what they are.

Both these amazing people are clearly "connectors" in the way that they have united millions of people in a common quest to make our world a healthier, more sustainable place to be, but Greta is also a powerful "activist" and "evangelist" in support of climate action. David Attenborough, on the other hand, uses his "specialist" knowledge and "explorer" curiosity to intrigue and inspire us to protect and enhance all aspects of the living world from ecosystems, through biodiversity to climate.

Our global world order

It would be remiss to talk about connection without referencing humanity's efforts to connect at the highest levels of government.

The United Nations: "peace, dignity and equality on a healthy planet"

As World War II was about to end in 1945, nations were in ruins, and the world wanted peace. Representatives of 50 countries gathered at the United Nations Conference on International Organization in San Francisco, California, from 25 April to 26 June 1945. For the next two months, they proceeded to draft and then sign the UN Charter, creating a new international organisation, the United Nations, which, it was hoped, would prevent another world war like the one they had just lived through.[8]

The purpose now declared by the UN is "Peace, dignity and equality on a healthy planet". Since its inception, unsurprisingly, the UN has faced many challenges and seen several reforms. It is widely seen as a beacon of hope for a brighter future and was instrumental in 2000 in launching the Millennium Development Goals (MDGs), a commitment to achieve international development in areas such as poverty reduction, gender equality and public health. Whilst uniting the world in a laudable quest, the MDGs were only partly successful and consequently and necessarily paved the way for the 2015 UN Sustainable Development Goals (SDGs).

It was at Christmastime in 2014 that I first saw a pre-agreement draft of the SDGs. I had just finished writing the final chapter of *Designing the Purposeful Organization* and had closed with the suggestion that the "conditions for success" described therein, including a powerful purpose and compelling vision, could and should be applied to the whole world. So

22 What is *beyond* sustainability? The six aspirations

here I was in December 2014, reading the best Christmas present the world could ever have (in my humble opinion), a blueprint for a better world. I immediately began writing *Designing the Purposeful World – the Sustainable Development Goals as a Blueprint for Humanity*, which was published by Routledge in 2018.[9]

There is little doubt in my mind that the UN and the SDGs have been a force for tremendous good in the world. Yet with wars now raging in Ukraine, in the Middle East and so many other troubled parts of our world, I can't but think there must be a better way.

It seems that UN Secretary-General António Guterres agrees. Since the beginning of his term in 2017, he has been striving for reform in the areas of development, management, peace and security. Readers can explore the progress of reforms on the UN Reforms page.[10]

> With the structural aspects of the reforms now well consolidated, it is imperative to keep the foot in the pedal to achieve the cultural change we need for greater collaboration across pillars and tangible results for people on the ground".
>
> António Guterres

Just as I was inspired when world leaders signed onto the SDGs in New York in September 2015, I fully expect further progress from the United Nations in years to come. After all, the number of people working at the United Nations has risen steadily in recent years – from just under 110,000 in 2018 to over 125,000 in 2022. This is truly a global army of people all seeking to make our world a better place.

From my side, I became an active participant in the United Nations Association (UK) and was a branch chair from 2015 to 2022. If there were two things, I would hope for regarding the UN, they would be as follows:

1. Quite simply more time allocated between world leaders to listen compassionately to each other in an attempt to understand different perspectives and work towards securing a better, fairer and more peaceful world for us all.
2. A relocating of UN HQ away from the United States to a country that would be seen to be more neutral on the world stage. For example, in recent years, Iceland has been a beacon for peace in the world. Somewhere like this might be a precursor for a different and more inclusive global culture, acceptable to the broad range of governments.

The European Union

As an Englishman, having experienced the UK's departure from the EU at the start of 2020, I also want to note the powerful work that has been done in recent years to connect countries within wider geographical regions such as Asia, Africa and (as an example for discussion below) Europe. Such collaborations are not without their challenges, but they do force a connecting narrative in support of a brighter future.

The European Union was formed when the Maastricht Treaty[11] came into force in 1993 and was subsequently incorporated as an international law juridical person upon entry into force of the Treaty of Lisbon in 2009. However, in a similar vein to the United Nations as discussed above, the roots of the EU can be traced back to a desire for peace and unity and an antidote to extreme nationalism following two world wars. Of notable influence was "The European Federalist Movement", founded in Milan in 1943 by a group of activists led by Altiero Spinelli propagated European integration.

Please read with interest further facts and figures about the European Union at its website (https://european-union.europa.eu/principles-countr ies-history/key-facts-and-figures/structure_en), including how in 1951 six countries (Belgium, France, Germany, Italy, Luxembourg and the Netherlands) founded the European Coal and Steel Community. In 1958, this became known as the European Economic Community (EEC), and its name was changed to the European Union in 1993 (as mentioned above). Over the years, 22 more countries joined the original six. On 1 February 2020, the United Kingdom left the EU. The EU currently has 27 Member States and 24 official languages.

The EU is not without its challenges and critics, but it has been a key driver of relative peace in Europe since World War II. For this reason alone, I was saddened to see the UK in 2020 notably withdraw its membership consequent to the so-called "Brexit" referendum. It is, however, encouraging to see tensions from that time being eased due to improved diplomacy and leadership from the likes of King Charles and Rishi Sunak. Hopefully, the UK will maintain harmonious relations with Europe and perhaps draw even closer in the years ahead.

Simply put, when nation-states connect, build strong relationships with each other and can discuss the most effective means to peaceful and democratic governance, the chances of delivering our "brighter future" are greatly enhanced.

24 What is *beyond* sustainability? The six aspirations

A series of personal encounters

As I have hinted above, the aspiration of a connected world is huge and brimming with opportunity. It embraces the good and innovative use of technology, connected and wise government, collaboration between businesses as well as love, compassion and kindness between all of us and all of life.

I really can't overemphasise that, whilst there are amazing things happening all over the world due to government, big business and world-famous celebrities, the real power of our collective journey to a more connected world lies in the hands of billions of ordinary people like you and me. In support of this, I offer the following case studies from my personal experience. You are probably not aware of them, and you may not regard them as the most earth-shattering stories. But that's the whole point.

These are stories to which I feel a personal connection. They involve people who have been, to some greater or lesser extent, a part of my life. They are all examples of people working hard to deliver a better world, beyond sustainability. As you read these stories, ask yourself what difference these people and organisations are making. Try to think beyond the immediate outcomes. Think about the effect they are having on supply chains. Think about how the people directly affected by their efforts are in their turn affecting others. Think about the way they set an example to others.

We naturally and vastly underestimate the effect we all have on our brighter future. This is my conclusion and one that gives me hope that our brighter future will be delivered way faster than any of us can imagine.

PERSONAL ENCOUNTER 1.1 – PHIL CLOTHIER, JOHN CAMPBELL AND AIESEC: "CONNECTING ALL YOUNG PEOPLE ON THE PLANET"

Towards the end of 2015, not long after the world leaders signed onto the UN SDGs, I was walking towards Harlow Carr Gardens in Harrogate with my friend and colleague, John Campbell, founder of our consultancy Primeast. His phone rang, he glanced at the screen and decided to answer it. After a minute or two, all I heard him say was "I'll ask him". He hung up and explained that Phil Clothier, then CEO of Barrett Values Centre and a dear mutual friend, had just explained that he had been asked to facilitate a workshop for about 500 young leaders at the UN Headquarters in New York. He wanted to know if John and I could work with him on the assignment.

Both our diaries were pretty manic in the run-up to Christmas, so we were amazed to discover that, with a bit of flexing, we could both make the trip. The event was being run by AIESEC,[12] the world's largest youth-led youth leadership development organisation.

Founded in 1948, AIESEC is a non-governmental and not-for-profit organisation entirely run by youth for youth. It is the largest organisation of its kind in the world and now has an alumnus of over a million leaders around the world. Pertinent to this book, it is a powerful force for connection, allowing young people to develop their leadership potential through practical experiences of many kinds, including internships, volunteering opportunities, and more.

What followed was bit of a whirlwind. John and I worked with Phil to facilitate a workshop to help AIESEC plan a means "to bring the UN Sustainable Development Goals to the attention of every young person on the planet". Furthermore, I was able to demonstrate a workshop to the full conference of over 400 young leaders that I had already been running successfully in Europe to raise the profile of the SDGs with groups of all ages and disciplines.

This experience and countless initiatives around the world are connecting people in a spirit of love and compassion, thereby encouraging interest and involvement in the delivery of our "brighter future".

In particular, I'd like to celebrate here and now the work of Phil Clothier who was instrumental in securing the support of John and I in this work. I know that Phil's unashamed driver of all he does is "Love". You'll also hear more about Phil's influence on the world in Chapter 6 when we explore the aspiration of Profound Wisdom. Phil has recently left Barrett Values Centre to establish a new consultancy, Amcara, with his friend and colleague, Tor Eneroth. The words on their new homepage[13] are telling:

Wellbeing for all Life!
Creating a sustainable world today, tomorrow, together.

Consider how, in the above personal encounter, so many connections are playing out. There were personal connections between John, Phil and me, as friends and colleagues. There was deep trust in Phil, to follow his lead with little questioning to go to New York for the UN Youth Action Summit.

26 What is *beyond* sustainability? The six aspirations

There is the power of AIESEC to connect thousands of young people together to learn and experience leadership. There is the power of United Nations to connect nations in the quest for peace and the SDGs to provide a focus that we can all connect to. And finally, the determination of those at the Summit to connect and involve literally "all young people".

Never before has the world been so well-connected. Imagine how difficult, if not impossible, it would have been to make such profound changes without the technology we have available to us, technology that we take for granted like mobile phones, the Internet, jet planes and conference centres. Nor would such changes take place without the love of a brighter future and compassion for those who suffer the most in our world.

Hold these thoughts as you join me for this next personal encounter, once again involving John Campbell.

PERSONAL ENCOUNTER 1.2 – THE SPIRIT OF HUMANITY FORUM: "LOVE AND COMPASSION IN CHANGE"

In 2014, I was asked to participate in the second Spirit of Humanity Forum in Reykjavik,[14] Iceland. I was part of a small delegation from Primeast, including John Campbell mentioned above, alongside colleagues from Barrett Values Centre, including its founder, Richard Barrett who was a keynote speaker.

The Spirit of Humanity Forum had started as an idea from a group in the Gulf State of Oman. Given its role as a peacemaker in the region, it seemed an obvious place for bringing together leaders to explore the role of spiritual values in decision-making. Iceland was also on the horizon for this work which was further explored by the Brahma Kumaris and Education for Peace. The name was chosen to reflect the deep exploration of the connection between our inner spiritual values and the world around us. Those who helped establish Iceland as the home of the Spirit of Humanity Forum were Ingibjörg Sólrún Gísladóttir, former Foreign Minister of Iceland, Jón Gnarr, then Mayor of Reykjavik and the late Sigrún Olsen and Thor Barðdal, who were directors of the Brahma Kumaris in Iceland. With the support of the City of Reykjavik, the first Spirit of Humanity Forum took place in 2012.

The focus of the second Forum was to explore the potential of love and compassion in bringing about effective change through governance and leadership. The aim was to begin to reconceptualise systemic change, especially in fields such as education, health, culture, science, business, politics and peacebuilding. The positive energy of love and compassion was regarded as one of the deepest and most enduring aspects of human nature. Taking this potential to be key for a sustainable economy, a loving society and a healthy environment, the Forum in Reykjavik in 2014 made an explicit call for love and compassion in action.

There was a powerful agenda of speakers and workshops, and I was privileged to share some thoughts from the book I was writing at that time, *Designing the Purposeful Organization*. I offered the PrimeFocus framework (Figure 1.2) as a simple but robust framework depicting eight "conditions" required for any change at any scale. We will further discuss the opportunity this framework presents in the concluding chapter of this book.

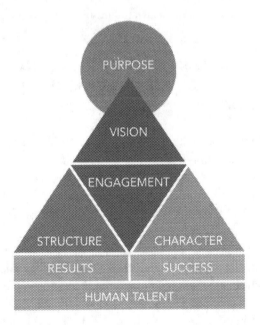

Figure 1.2 PrimeFocus™.

> I include this experience as a personal encounter exemplifying once again the value of love, compassion, collaboration and connection. Spirit of Humanity is by no means the only vehicle for this work, nor am I placing it on any particular pedestal of greatness. We will all have examples of movements and institutions doing great work to promote a brighter future for our world. They are all worthy of their place in the great ecosystem of planetary evolution.

Connection can be large in scale, and it can also be deep, very deep, involving intimacy, compassion and true love. The scale of my next personal encounter is no less profound. The truth is, throughout the world, people draw on enormous strength to deal with illness and tragedy within their homes and neighbourhoods. When the going gets tough, heroes emerge to make life as bright as it can be for those around them.

As you read, you will doubtless be reminded of people in your own life who are in difficult situations and others who are responding with compassion and determination. Perhaps you are personally involved in some way and have had to withdraw from one act of service to deal with priorities in another. Somehow, in the midst of challenges, we find purpose and hope.

PERSONAL ENCOUNTER 1.3 – NICK AND LINDA: "PERSONAL PURPOSE THROUGH CONNECTION"

For ten years until her recent retirement, my wife Frances worked as a careers advisor at Ripon Grammar School and then as an independent careers consultant. During this time, she enjoyed working closely with Linda, another careers advisor. At the young age of just 53 years old, Linda retired and was later diagnosed with early onset of Alzheimer's disease.

The friendship between Linda and Frances grew stronger, partly because of the connection they shared through a local "Rock up and Sing" choir which Linda continued for a few years after her retirement.

Linda's husband, Nick, also joined the choir, and I met him at some of their concerts where I came along to support and be entertained.

It wasn't long until Nick chose to retire from his work as a senior civil servant to care for Linda. Always positive and smiling, Nick devoted himself to Linda's well-being. At first, Frances and I would join in with them on local walks. We even had a wonderful holiday in Northumberland where Linda could really enjoy being on beaches that were expansive and easy to navigate.

Sadly, Linda is no longer able to go on walks, having lost the ability to sufficiently co-ordinate the movement of her legs. Nick still cares for Linda at their home, with the support of family members and now a live-in friend and carer, who just happens to be the mother of their son's girlfriend!

For a short break from caring for Linda, Nick occasionally calls us to arrange a visit to one of our local pubs. We enjoy, usually light-hearted, conversation and occasionally some of the challenges of looking after Linda.

On one occasion, I shared with Nick, my admiration for his positivity and dedication. He confessed that it isn't always easy, but also his connection to Linda gives him such a strong sense of purpose in life and the energy to do what he needs to do. He also commented on the connection he has made to some of the charities that have helped him and Linda over recent years and a further sense of purpose to support them in whatever way he is able in the future.

Speaking of his overall experience of caring for Linda, Nick had this to say:

> I feel that the past few years, which could be regarded as the saddest we have experienced, have allowed me to find some inner strength and that I will look back on them eventually as the most rewarding experience of my life. The more I have given, the more I get back.

One thing I struggled with in writing this book was knowing which of our six aspirations to place each encounter under. The next story could easily have been told under the banner of "abundance" or "opportunity". For me, it demonstrates connections between people and the power of love and compassion. Note also the ripple effect and the joy of unintended consequences.

30 What is *beyond* sustainability? The six aspirations

PERSONAL ENCOUNTER 1.4 – NEVILLE BEVIS AND WILSON JOHN: "LOVE ONE DAY AT A TIME"

It was 1999 and my son David shared over dinner that his biology teacher, Neville Bevis, was leaving to travel to Malawi, then the poorest country in the world, to work to support orphaned infants who had lost their parents, often due to HIV, and did not have a family structure to support them. For 17 years, Neville and his wife Rosemary (now deceased) ran the Open Arms Infant Home in Blantyre,[15] the commercial centre of Malawi. Their wonderful team of local people and volunteers gave care to infants from birth to two years old or until they could be placed back in the villages from whence they came. Their mission was to provide "love one day at a time" in a part of the world that so desperately needed it.

A minority of children, for a variety of reasons, could not be placed back in their communities and so were housed at Open Arms until they were four. At this point, if there was still no prospect of caring for them in their villages, they were found accommodation with foster parents, sponsored by the charity's donors, comprising individuals and corporations.

Inspired by Neville, Rosemary and their teams in Malawi and UK, and by David's enthusiasm, I began raising money for the charity, through speaking events, exhibitions of my paintings and even by writing the life story of a local businessman. A few years later I felt called to visit Malawi to witness the work of Open Arms first-hand.

On my arrival at the infant home in Blantyre, a four-year-old boy came running across the yard towards me. "Hi", he said, "my name's Wilson".

"Wow" I replied, "my name's Wilson too! We must be brothers!"

He hugged me, we laughed for a while and then Wilson showed me around his home.

There is much more to this story but, for the purpose of this book, suffice to say, this is a personal example of the power of love, compassion and connection playing out in a wonderful way – connection through my son David, to Neville, to Open Arms, to Malawi, to

> Wilson John. Connections like these encouraged me to visit Malawi several times, I visited schools, hospitals, spoke at conferences, worked as a consultant to organisations such as Standard Bank and the British Council and even set up a small business so that local people could work in the field of leadership development and continue to facilitate the development of a brighter future for local organisations and those they served.
>
> To me, my Malawian adventure is a personal playing out of the power of connection. As we notice and respond to life's so-called "coincidences" amazing things happen. We achieve very little in isolation but so much happens when our consciousness flows in the wider system we call humanity.
>
> I haven't been to Malawi for about a decade now, but I suspect the adventure continues. Neville, now retired (well sort of), paid a visit back to Harrogate. We met up in the Harrogate Tap, a great pub, next door to the train station. He's still in touch with Wilson John and shared ideas on how best to support his growth. Wilson is embarking on a career as a videographer and spreading the word of his work by working part-time in a local barber's shop. He is also working on a farm owned by Neville which also contributes to his earnings.

I hope my next encounter will prompt reflection on connection in the world of work. Most of us spend a significant amount of our time here. Hopefully, we enjoy a journey of service and meaning. Over a lifetime, we probably connect, one way or another, with tens of thousands of people. Sadly, and perhaps necessarily, we forget most of them. Occasionally, we bump into someone at a conference, a party or just passing in the street, and the thought "Where do I know you from?" goes through our minds. Sometimes we ask them and sometimes we don't. Either way, such encounters can serve to remind us, once more, of the power of connection.

My career journey falls into two neat halves. The years 1972–2000 were spent as an engineer and manager in the electricity industry. I look back with fond memories of dealing with faults and getting people's electricity back on supply and then leading vast change programmes. One such programme introduced me to the power of leadership and cultural change and prompted a career shift into consultancy right at the turn of the century.

32 What is *beyond* sustainability? The six aspirations

PERSONAL ENCOUNTER 1.5 – JOHN CAMPBELL: "A GLOBAL NETWORK OF CHANGE AGENTS"

In 2001, I was asked by the Confederation of British Industry to speak at a conference on Purposeful Leadership. John Campbell, founder and (then) managing director of Primeast, was also speaking and invited me to meet up before the conference to "compare notes". There was a great deal of synergy between our messages and subsequently John asked me to deliver a couple of projects on behalf of Primeast. One thing led to another and the following year, in February 2002, John and the board of Primeast invited me to lead the business.

Primeast has been in operation since 1987, and I guess its story is not dissimilar to many other organisations. It has always served its clients with purposeful leadership and high performance through teamwork. To do this effectively, the company has drawn on a growing network of trainers, facilitators and coaches, spread across the globe.

On occasions, we were asked by global corporates if we could deliver programmes in some of the weirdest and most remote locations on the planet and often in the local languages. The answer was always "yes we can", and the challenge then was to go to our network, identify suitable local practitioners and sometimes draw on their network in turn.

Today, Primeast takes a great deal of time and care to manage its faculty of professionals, keeping them up to date with our latest thinking and methods and, as best we can, feeling connected to the business.

The second Primeast example of connection that I'm especially proud of is with the many thousands of participants who attend our programmes each year. We share with them powerful insights and methods to help them become better leaders, and many of them keep in touch for years to come. Of course, we don't always get to hear about the way they, in turn, connect with their colleagues and friends to share their learning. For every past participant who reappears on our radar seeking further support, it is sobering to know that there are probably thousands more who don't and yet continue to connect in a positive way beyond our network.

As with many of the case studies in this book, the people involved with Primeast, its clients, suppliers and employees rarely stop to appreciate the power of human connection that makes our work possible. It will be the same for many of the organisations you are familiar with, and it is my encouragement (as throughout this book) to notice, encourage and celebrate this connection wherever it manifests in our world.

Speaking of bumping into people from our past prompts me to share another story of meeting someone who had been a participant at one of my workshops. I am always delighted to meet people I have worked with later in their lives, especially if our work together has been helpful.

PERSONAL ENCOUNTER 1.6 – OLGA RAK: "BE THE CHANGE YOU WANT TO SEE IN THE WORLD"

I first met Olga when I was running an online workshop in support of young people's careers. I was sharing thoughts on how to contribute to a purposeful world. I explained how purpose works – that it is a feeling caused by the energetic reaction between who we think we are and how we see our world. I talked about making shifts in our life-construct that would build on this feeling and strengthen our purpose.

You can imagine my delight when one of the attendees posted the following on LinkedIn. Her original post was in French, so please forgive me for using the auto-translation with a few minor edits to make it more accessible:

It is with pride that I show green and blue colours on my profile picture today (colours of the Swiss Green Liberal Party[16]). Convinced that even if each individual contribution counts, it is together that we create things with even more impact. Four years ago, I followed a webinar by Clive Wilson, "How you can contribute to a purposeful world". He made us think about the causes that awaken emotions in us, and especially those that make us want to take action. The

34 What is *beyond* sustainability? The six aspirations

basis for reflection is simple, but so relevant: the Sustainable Development Goals established by the United Nations. Here are the objectives that drive me the most today (although I must admit that all the objectives resonate with me): SDG3 Good Health and Well-Being; SDG5 Gender Equality; SDG7 Clean and Affordable Energy; SDG12 Responsible Consumption and Production; SDG13 Climate Action; SDG16 Peace, Justice and Strong Institutions. In my professional life, it is SDG16 that occupies my daily life and, in particular, the "16.6 Build effective, accountable and transparent institutions at all levels". In terms of my civic engagement, it is especially SDG13 that drives me to action against climate change. And you, what causes awaken in you your inner flame and make you want to take action?

Naturally, I was curious to learn more about the shifts in Olga's career. So, I contacted her on LinkedIn and arranged to have a video catch-up.

I listened as Olga shared how she knew that she would have to change something after the webinar. She had a real passion for sustainable development, justice and peace. She decided to become a candidate for the Swiss National Council, as a representative of the Green Liberal Party of Switzerland, which she enthusiastically described as having strategies aligned to her beliefs in both environmentalism and liberal economics. She had this to say about her move into politics:

> I like the quote "be the change you want to see in the world". After adjusting all my individual actions that can impact the climate issues, I clearly understood that I have to spread the change around me. People often say that individual effort is insufficient until all the society changes, and then they blame the politicians who do nothing for this. This pushed me to go into politics and embody this change. The Green Liberal Party slogan is "Courage to act", act for a healthy planet for the next generations, act to create our future, and I am eager to act now.

Olga is lively, passionate and purpose-driven, and I know she will be a powerful influencer for change in the years to come. I shall be following, supporting and celebrating her journey.

Chapter summary – the power of six

Who are the individuals or organisations you have come across during your life's journey who are making the world a more positively connected place to be in? Who are the ones who continually raise the bar or set precedents for connection, compassion, love and kindness?

Make a note of your top six (notice), preferably those where you have some kind of personal connection. If you're not still in touch, why not check them out online and perhaps even post a suitable case study of your own on social media (celebrate) with your own words of encouragement? If you're struggling (which I doubt very much) then check out some of the cases in this chapter and simply post their work online.

And what about you? Make a note of six things you're already doing to connect positively with others. How do compassion, love and kindness play out in your own life? Then make a note of six more things you'd like to do in the future – preferably in your diary on the date you're going to make a start.

Notes

1 Wilson, C. A. 2023. Poem "Connection" by Author.
2 Wikipedia, 2024. History of Google: https://en.wikipedia.org/wiki/History_of_Google.
3 National Poetry Day, 2024. Poem by Anon: https://nationalpoetryday.co.uk/poem/for-want-of-a-nail/.
4 Attributed (unrecorded) to Jimi Hendrix.
5 Wilson, C. A. 2022. "Leading a Purposeful Life" by Author: www.lulu.com/shop/clive-wilson/leading-a-purposeful-life/paperback/product-9r5deq.html?q=clive+wilson+leading+a+purposeful+life&page=1&pageSize=4 (also available as eBook free of charge from author).
6 Wikipedia, 2024. Steve Stills "Love the one you're with": https://en.wikipedia.org/wiki/Love_ the_One_You%27re_With
7 Boldt, L. G. 2009. "Zen and the Art of Making a Living": www.penguinrandomhouse.ca/books/305451/zen-and-the-art-of-making-a-living-by-laurence-g-boldt/9781101202685
8 United Nations, 2024. History of the UN: www.un.org/en/about-us/history-of-the-un
9 Wilson, 2018. "Designing the Purposeful World": www.routledge.com/Designing-the-Purposeful-World-The-Sustainable-Development-Goals-as-a-Blueprint/Wilson/p/book/9780815381327

36 What is *beyond* sustainability? The six aspirations

10 United Nations, 2024. UN Reforms page: https://reform.un.org/
11 Wikipedia, 2024. Maastricht Treaty: https://en.wikipedia.org/wiki/Maastricht_Treaty
12 AIESEC, 2024. AIESEC: https://aiesec.org/
13 Amcara, 2024. Amcara: www.amcara.life/
14 Spirit of Humanity Forum, 2024. Spirit of Humanity Forum: www.sohforum.org/previous-forums/iceland/2nd-forum-2014/
15 Open Arms Malawi, 2024. Open Arms Infant Homes: www.openarmsmalawi.org/
16 Wikipedia, 2024. Green Liberal Party of Switzerland: https://en.wikipedia.org/wiki/Green_Liberal_Party_of_Switzerland

The freedom of peace 2

Peace

With an eerie crack
The last bullet was shot
And the last casualty
Bit the dust of the battlefield

The news came on X
That the war was over
What happens next?
Silence and then …

In the distance a bird sang
More sweetly than ever
And then a bell rang
From a church in the East
And another to the North
Like an overture

Then tears of joy and of sorrow
Men ran to embrace each other
No war
Just a new tomorrow

We can play football again
Go back to work again

DOI: 10.4324/9781003428121-4

38 What is *beyond* sustainability? The six aspirations

Holiday in each other's countries again
Spend time with our families again

Make sure this never happens again
Never ever again[1]

Where do we find peace?

Over the years, I have spent a great deal of time contemplating why there is so much violence in the world and what might be done to find peace. This usually follows hearing of violence somewhere in the world – the outbreak or continuation of a war between nations and within nations, or tragic news of gun or knife crime in our communities.

But I'd like to begin with a contemplation.

> ### ACTIVITY: WHERE DO YOU FIND PEACE?
>
> Close your eyes and think about your own experience of peace. Where have you been able to find peace? Think as widely and creatively as you can. Make a list in your journal of at least ten ways you have found peace. What conclusions can you make from this exercise?

Here is my list of ten, in no particular order:

1. Sitting in meditation or prayer, connecting deliberately with a higher level of consciousness.
2. Watching an animal, insect, bird or flower and appreciating its beauty.
3. Walking in a forest.
4. Sitting on a rock beside the sea, watching the waves come into the shore and returning.
5. Sitting with my wife beside a wood-burning stove at the end of a satisfying day.
6. In a busy market watching the traders have fun with their customers.
7. On a long drive in my campervan listening to my favourite music.
8. Hearing of the successes of my colleagues and clients.
9. In a hot bath with scented oils and candles.
10. Sitting in my garden in the sunshine.

What did I learn from making my list? Something about being present to what's going on around me. Something about simplicity. Something that isn't hard to find if, in the words of John Lennon, we "give peace a chance". Something inherently valuable, something that all of life deserves to experience more than just occasionally.

A worthy goal and a powerful enabler

Not only is peace a worthy goal in and of itself, but it is a contributory enabler of all our other aspirations as well. Conflict at any level is a barrier to connection between nations, communities and even between individuals in organisations, teams and families. It is a barrier to the production and flow of services and resources between communities. By its very nature, it harms the well-being of individuals and communities and in all-too-oft extreme cases takes human lives in vast quantities, leaving families grieving, angry, stressed and far from well. It takes away opportunity from people and nations, whether to participate in international programmes or simply by stopping people from encouraging and facilitating personal growth. Finally, the tendency to react and over-react in times of conflict is about as far from wisdom as we can get.

I confess that, from the outset, writing this chapter filled me with trepidation. I recently spoke at an event on this topic and shared graphs from Our World in Data[2] and Steven Pinker's[3] books (see below) showing the long-term decline in violence of most kinds. Yet close to home in Europe, we are right now experiencing a bloody war that has already taken the lives of hundreds of thousands of soldiers on both sides of the Ukraine conflict and far too many civilians.

And, in October 2023 we saw the horrific conflict in Israel and Palestine. Like many, I watched with horror the savage attacks in Israel and the brutal reprisals in Gaza. It made me ask the question, "In and amongst all of this, where is peace?" Then I noticed a few hopeful reports of Jews and Muslims coming together in support of each other and in a cry for peace. How different are such acts of love and kindness to the reports of violence in the region and in cities around the world. It also made me think again of Vijay Mehta's wonderful book *How Not to Go to War*. I say more about this in my "personal encounter" with Vijay below. It made me wonder if this and other violence could have been prevented if the warring parties had previously established Departments for Peace in their respective governments and if,

40 What is *beyond* sustainability? The six aspirations

knowing of the potential for violence, they had done more to mitigate it. More of that below.

And there are conflicts elsewhere in the world – too many to mention.

The situation in Ukraine, at the time of writing, is delicately balanced. I watched NATO convene to discuss Ukraine's ascension to its membership, and I listened intently to accounts of the seriousness of the decision-making, not taken lightly but involving thousands of professionals engaged in such conversations. They seem genuinely intent on defending the Ukraine nation from extra-state aggression, securing a lasting peace and avoiding escalation.

The purpose of this book is certainly not to allocate blame, point any fingers or speculate on the causes of particular wars. I keep reminding myself that this text is about aligning the peoples of this world to a brighter and, as far as this chapter is concerned, more peaceful future. I have no intention to back-edit my words, but I do hope that, by the time this book goes to print, there will, once again, be peace in Europe, the Middle East and elsewhere. Also, that the longer-term trends will be towards peace – a total absence of war and decreasing violence of all kinds.

Returning to my event audience, I compared long-term trends in violence to examining the stock market. As you zoom into the monthly, daily or hour-by-hour fluctuations, the picture looks more and more haphazard. Yet, financial planners have been able to rely on 4% growth over any ten-year period in order to provide reliable pensions for people in their retirement.

Just as there was serious contemplation and dialogue after World War II that led to the birth of the United Nations, I trust there will be serious dialogue following all conflicts to put in place systems and processes to facilitate the journey to a brighter, more peaceful world.

There are many enablers of peace in the world. Some of them are covered in our other chapters. To name a few, we can consider:

- Deep, meaningful and constructive dialogue between leaders and individuals (Chapter 1 on Connection)
- Healthy, thriving communities and ecosystems again causing less scarcity and friction between communities (see Chapter 3 on Vitality)
- Carefully and compassionately managed abundance of food, water, energy, services and wealth giving communities less reason to fight (Chapter 4 on Abundance)
- Education, especially for girls and the enhancement of life skills (see Chapter 5 on Opportunity)

The freedom of peace **41**

- More involvement of women in leadership (this chapter and Chapter 5 on Opportunity)
- A shared purpose and vision of a peaceful world (this chapter and this whole book)
- A rational examination of data in terms of what enables peace and what causes conflict so humanity can advance peaceful systems and cultures (this chapter)
- The conscious and progressive development of wisdom in our world and especially for leaders (Chapter 6 on Wisdom and Part III on further exploration in the Wisdom Code)
- The establishment of Departments for Peace in every government, local, regional, national and international.

ACTIVITY

What other enablers of peace can you think of and who do you know that is working towards this aspiration? Make notes in your journal.

Conflict is a major obstacle to positive evolution. And yet, research identifies that violence is declining over the very long term. In this chapter, we identify the trends and celebrate the work of peacemakers in various guises. We also explore what it means to find peace in a troubled world by starting with ourselves.

ACTIVITY: CHECKING OUT THE DATA

There is an abundance of data available on trends relating to violence – see the "War and Peace" pages on the "Our World in Data" journal online. Make notes in your journal about your conclusions.

The work of Steven Pinker

I don't know of anyone alive today who encourages us more to look at the data surrounding the decline in violence than Steven Pinker.

42 What is *beyond* sustainability? The six aspirations

I came across Steven Pinker when I was exploring the UN Sustainable Development Goals[4] for my book *Designing the Purposeful World.*[5] I was curious to know whether the world was becoming a more violent place, as many of us might think when we tune into our national and international news stations or read the newspapers. I discovered that, quite to the contrary, the world is becoming a vastly safer place to live with violent deaths of all sorts declining since records began.

Pinker confirms this in his book *The Better Angels of our Nature – Why Violence Has Declined* (2011), and it is also borne out in data held in the "War and Peace" pages of the "Our World in Data" website. This notwithstanding the current conflicts described above.

Pinker's 2021 book, *Rationality: What It Is, Why It Seems Scarce, Why It Matters*, builds on this advice for all of us to check the data. "Rationality" encourages us to be neither optimistic nor pessimistic. Simply, we must act on facts, and the facts generally tell us that the world is getting better in terms of long-term trends and on most fronts.

Global Peace Index and the concept of Positive Peace

Much of the data discussed above is "badged up" as the decline of violence. So I became increasingly interested in the implied positivity of this movement.

The Global Peace Index[6] or GPI was founded by Steve Killelea, an Australian technology entrepreneur and philanthropist. It is produced by the Institute for Economics and Peace, a global think tank dedicated to developing metrics to analyse peace and to quantify its economic benefits. The GPI measures a country's level of Negative Peace using three domains of peacefulness.

The first domain, Ongoing Domestic and International Conflict, uses six statistical indicators to investigate the extent to which countries are involved in internal and external conflicts, as well as their role and duration of involvement in conflicts.

The second domain evaluates the level of harmony or discord within a nation; 11 indicators broadly assess what might be described as Societal Safety and Security. The assertion is that low crime rates, minimal terrorist activity and violent demonstrations, harmonious relations with neighbouring countries, a stable political scene and a small proportion of the population being internally displaced or made refugees can be equated with peacefulness.

The freedom of peace   43

Six further indicators are related to a country's Militarisation – reflecting the link between a country's level of military build-up and access to weapons and its level of peacefulness, both domestically and internationally. Comparable data on military expenditure as a percentage of GDP and the number of armed service officers per head are gauged, as are financial contributions to UN peacekeeping missions.

The Institute for Economics and Peace – and the eight Pillars of Positive Peace

Note how, despite the badging of the GPI, the measurements are predominantly of violence and machinery of violence. I say this not to imply criticism. The work of GPI is extremely valuable. However, I became increasingly curious to find more information on how peace, and pertinently the enablers

Figure 2.1 The Pillars of Positive Peace.

44 What is *beyond* sustainability? The six aspirations

of peace, can be defined and measured. I was encouraged to learn about the work of the Institute for Economics and Peace and its eight "Pillars of Positive Peace".[7]

I love the fact that the eight pillars are all things we can work consciously towards. In the main, they are also expressed positively, in line with the objectives of this book. The only pillar that is expressed in the form of a negative is "low levels of corruption". I think I understand the reasoning. The pillar is something we can all easily envisage. At the same time, I became curious and looked up "the opposite of corruption". I found out that it was about the following: honesty, decency, integrity, probity, righteousness, virtue, character, dependability, justness and scrupulousness. Now that sounds like a (positively) brighter future "beyond sustainability". What's more, it opens the door for us to "notice, encourage and celebrate" more and more people working for peace.

The pillars as a set also resonate in the way they are totally fractal: it's possible to see them playing out at any scale, from the global order to personal behaviours. Consider how any one of us might

- Vote for wise government
- Share resources with others
- Share useful information
- Build good relationships with our neighbours
- Develop ourselves and others
- Acknowledge and facilitate the rights of others
- Be fair and honest in our dealings with others
- Adopt fair and productive business practices

ACTIVITY: GROW A STRONGER "VISION OF HUMANITY"

Take time to explore the Vision of Humanity website, especially the page on the Eight Pillars of Positive Peace. Then find the Positive Peace case studies brochure (at the same website). Read the case studies from Uganda, Ethiopia, The Philippines and Australia. As you do so, make a note of how many of the eight pillars are positively impacted by the work described. Make your own notes in your journal before scrolling down to discover my conclusions. Also note how you could take these examples and leverage the learning for your own action plan.

My own inspiration from these case studies

Kakuba Literacy Project, Kampala, Uganda

It has been said by many commentators that education is a key enabler of peace. I have read studies over the years that conclude that communities where education, especially of women and girls, is a priority are less prone to violence and war.

I love the way Jude Kakuba made the connection between his involvement as a Rotarian, his desire to improve levels of literacy in a school in Kampala and the eight pillars of peace. He systematically applied each of the eight pillars for peace to his project which gave it a robust structure as well as stimulating creativity. I was also impressed by the measurement of the impact this project had – more than doubling attendance at the school and the number of students earning top grades.

At a personal level, this case study reminded me of the work I have done promoting the UN Sustainable Development Goals in Schools and Universities since their inception in 2015. It instantly reminded me of the powerful visions of peace described by young attendees at my workshops – especially the young girl who described happy children in a peaceful Syria (as told in my introduction to this book).

In terms of inspiring action, it has prompted me to contact schools and universities again to repeat the exercise with students, this time using the six aspirations as my "vision for humanity".

Peace 911, Paquibato, Davao City, Philippines

This case study emphasised for me the power of connection. It demonstrates how violence is facilitated when there is a dearth of health provision, nutrition and education. Irene Santiago worked with the Davao City local government to address these basic human needs as well as strengthening other community infrastructures such as transport and social services.

I was also struck that the case study describes how the most profound element of the Peace 911 project was the telephone hotline for local residents to call for assistance or information. Again, a powerful playing out of the pillar of "The Free Flow of Information", something that perhaps also fits within "Connection" and "Opportunity".

46 What is *beyond* sustainability? The six aspirations

Once more, measurable outcomes are key. Within just nine months, Peace 911 enabled the military to declare Paquibato "clear of the communist insurgency, an extraordinary outcome". The local Mayor consequently announced the expansion of the project to other districts.

For me, this reminded me of the work of Nathan Atkinson from Rethink Food, which I shall share in more detail in Chapter 4. In a nutshell, Nathan noticed that children could not be taught in his school if they arrived at the gates hungry. So, he did something about it.

I was also impressed how this work, which impacted several of our six aspirations for a brighter future, was branded definitely as a "Peace" project. Something that mattered a great deal to the communities involved at that time.

In terms of my own work, it made me realise the power of presenting the ideas in this book using whatever themes are important to those seeking to deploy them. At the time of writing these words in October 2023, I'm speaking at a conference on "Are we already in World War III? – Can a Roadmap for Peace Change Culture of War to Culture of Peace" as well as another where the students at a university in Asia are studying my earlier book *Designing the Purposeful Organisation* but are interested in the ideas from this latest text. We have agreed that the title for my workshop should be "Designing the Purposeful Organization – Aligning to a Brighter Future", thus coupling the ideas from the two texts.

The Ethiopian Positive Peace Ambassadors Programme

This is yet another powerful initiative prompted by an outbreak of violence, this time in Ethiopia's Tigray region. The conflict between federal and regional forces began in November 2020 and pushed tens of thousands of refugees into neighbouring Sudan causing a humanitarian crisis. The free programme was launched in February 2021 and again attracted the involvement of local Rotarians, as well as businesspeople, artists and entrepreneurs, and members of the Ethiopian Reconciliation Commission. It explicitly adopted the eight-pillars framework and centred on three webinars engaging hundreds of people.

The webinars resulted in over 130 peace projects and presentations submitted by participants. An outcome was the creation of a "Positive Peace Association", which creates a platform for Ethiopian Ambassadors on the ground to connect and further their work in Positive Peace.

The freedom of peace **47**

My personal inspiration from reading this case study was the reminder that we should never underestimate the potential power of a webinar. I have made a note to encourage those organising webinars on this book to provide space for follow-up. I am also reminded that, on each occasion, I should ask the question, "What did this webinar inspire you to do next?", and wherever possible to seek feedback later.

Matavai Cultural Arts Centre Positive Peace Workshop, New South Wales (NSW), Australia

Multicultural NSW (MNSW) in collaboration with the Institute of Economics and Peace (IEP) and Western Sydney University selected five NSW communities to deliver a project named "Positive Peace, Cultural Wellbeing and Youth Agency Initiative: Exploring peaceful solutions to living well in diverse communities". The project adapted IEP's Positive Peace Framework to each targeted community in order to foster cultural wellbeing. It also supported the development of community-led projects aiding the agency and resilience of each community. In turn, this contributed to broader social cohesion in an effort to counteract fear, hate, racism and societal discord.

By the time I got to this case study, my creative juices were running over. I had already contacted a very good and enthusiastic friend at a university to talk about running some new events, and this particular case study reminded me greatly of the work of Matt Walsh which I describe in Chapter 3 in my personal encounter on "Communities of Wellbeing". I'm now exploring even more ideas with Matt.

So, how did you get on?

I hope the last activity proved to be as creative for you as it did for me. I hope you've reached for your diary to book a meeting with someone to explore an idea or two. It just shows how one ten-page brochure can stimulate ideas for a wide audience. The IEP is the world's leading think tank dedicated to developing metrics to analyse peace and quantify its economic value. It does this by developing global and national indices, calculating the economic cost of violence, analysing country risk and understanding Positive Peace. IEP is best known for its annual publications the GPI, the Global Terrorism Index

48 What is *beyond* sustainability? The six aspirations

and the Positive Peace Report. IEP declares the following benefits towards the end of the brochure:

- 26 billion media impressions
- 8,600 news articles
- 152 countries
- 150 events

My suspicion is that this is just the tip of a very large iceberg. One that is growing by the actions already prompted for you and for me!

The (peaceful) sky is the limit

There is no end to the ways we can contribute to peace. As with all purposeful acts, we must trust that our perception of a context will speak to our hearts and, if we respond with integrity and authenticity, then I suggest we can trust that our actions will summon a brighter future at various moments in time and in various ways, including some that we may never discover. I rather suspect this was the case for Vedran Smajlovic[8] during the conflict in Sarajevo, when he played Adagio in G Minor for 22 days to mark the death of each of the 22 people killed in the street whilst queuing for bread. His story is told in the novel "The Cellist of Sarajevo" by Steven Galloway.

ACTIVITY

You can find several recordings of this piece of music on YouTube and elsewhere. Choose one and listen to it with your eyes closed. Visualise in your own way the scene of this being played in Sarajevo during the conflict. Then pause to contemplate the impacts Smajlovic's playing might have had at that moment and subsequently. He wasn't to know that his story would be retold in a novel or that his music would be played in remembrance. And he certainly wouldn't know how these consequential acts would inspire thousands of readers and listeners to contemplate the horrors of war and create an aspiration for peace.

The freedom of peace **49**

A great deal of Chapter 1 above relates to the connection and collaboration of world leaders at the United Nations and other international parliaments such as the European Union. To most of us, this seems very different, and we are left wondering what constructive work might be taking place a little closer to home. So, I hope you'll find encouragement in my "personal encounters" below and be inspired to identify your own peacemakers at the close of this chapter.

PERSONAL ENCOUNTER 2.1 – SATISH KUMAR: "WALKING FOR PEACE"

In the 1990s, my personal journey of "peace exploration" took me on a nine-year excursion into Buddhism, which I found most helpful in developing personal inner peace. During this time I read, what is still one of my favourite books, *No Destination* by Satish Kumar.[9] It is a fascinating autobiography of a man with a powerful love of life and of peace.

The book tells of a man who, amongst many other things, made a journey on foot from his home in India to the (then) four countries holding nuclear arms: Russia, France, UK and US. Along his journey, he met a woman who dearly wanted to go with him. Satish declined the prospect out of concern for the woman's safety. Instead, she gave him packets of tea to share with the world leaders concerned. It is an amazing story of just how much one man can achieve in expressing the longing so many of us have for a peaceful world.

I had the further good fortune to meet Satish at a Schumacher Lecture at Leeds University. His talk addressed so many of the challenges faced by humanity, and he answered a vast range of questions from his audience on many contentious topics. His responses were calm, considered and wise.

Since the 1990s, Satish keeps popping into my psyche, whether it is through reading the wonderful *Resurgence* magazine for which he served for many years as editor or through engaging with some of his subsequent books and videos on peace and ecology.

When we think of peacemakers, perhaps amazing leaders like Mahatma Gandhi spring to mind. But there are so many people advocating for peace

50 What is *beyond* sustainability? The six aspirations

in so many ways, including through the power of the arts, as my next encounter suggests.

PERSONAL ENCOUNTER 2.2 – THE POWER OF MUSIC: "PLAYING FOR CHANGE"

As a teenager attending an inner-city comprehensive school at Cross Green in Leeds, I spent many an evening dancing to loud music in the cellar disco at Halton Methodist Youth Club. I remember the power of this age of love, freedom and rock music. The call to action was clear in the words of the songs we moved to and the behaviours of those writing and singing them. Hearing the Beatles and John Lennon in particular chanting "All you need is love", "Give peace a chance", "You say you want a revolution" definitely encouraged me as a lifelong advocate for peace.

I remember making "peace cards" and posters and distributing them amongst friends. Even today, I have playlists of music that inspire me in the work I do in support of a better world. My family knows that "Clear White Light" by Lindisfarne must be played at my funeral. The very idea that something bright, shiny and powerful is "going to lead us on our way" remains the very essence of my personal spirituality. Indeed, you will discover that "The Clear White Light of Purpose" is the working title for a book on the power of spirituality I plan to write in 2025.

I was alive at the time of Woodstock and attended in spirit if not in person. I hope the world keeps singing a song of peace for all time.

More recently, I have been particularly impressed with the work of "Playing for Change".[10] This project brings together musicians from around the world and magically records them playing "in their own back yard", mixing their music with other musicians in different countries. As well as sounding amazing, this connection of musicians from different cultures advocating for peace and harmony is symbolic of exactly what the world needs.

In a similar vein and much closer to home, my own daughter, Helen, flautist with the Royal Liverpool Philharmonic Orchestra, staged a concert with other musicians on the theme of "People, Planet, Profit"[11] featuring her own arrangements and compositions

The freedom of peace **51**

and drawing attention, once again, to the prospect of a better world. I was honoured to participate in a small way in this performance by having my artwork featured on the projected images behind the musicians and in a small exhibition in a side room to raise funds for charity. Recordings of this performance are available on my YouTube channel.

Who do you know whose music or other art is inspiring a more peaceful world?

My next encounter could have easily featured under connection, vitality or wisdom. But I include it here under the banner of peace as I know firsthand the impact local small group sessions can have on the people who participate.

PERSONAL ENCOUNTER 2.3 – CHRIS BURFORD: "WE BURN BRIGHTER AS ONE"

There are thousands (if not more) of thought leaders and spiritual guides around the world who remind us all that peace actually begins within each one of us. Faith traditions encourage us to connect to one-ness in meditation or to "be still and know that I am God". The message is the same. As we escape from the duality of the material world and from psychological illusion, we begin to experience the peace of unity with all things. As we lessen our desire for material and psychological distractions, we begin to experience the peace of non-attachment. Bob Anderson touches on this subject in Chapter 6 as I share my personal encounter with his Wisdom.

For this personal encounter, I celebrate my friend, Chris Burford. I have known Chris for almost 20 years. We have worked together in the field of leadership development and have drawn closer by sharing our personal experiences of spirituality. Chris is an immensely compassionate man and has worked tirelessly for many years to support a charity dedicated to helping homeless people at St George's Crypt in Leeds.

However, the work of Chris that I especially wish to celebrate here is his provision of a small men's fellowship group which has become known as "Into Sacred Space". The method is simple but profound. About once a month, a small group of men assemble at Chris's home in Harrogate. We gather around a fire in (mostly) silence and each place a log on the fire, demonstrating that "we burn brighter as one". We then sit in candlelight and meditate for a few minutes. Next is a simple ceremony with a "talking stick". The ancient carved wooden baton is passed from man-to-man and we each, in turn, are given the space to say whatever we wish. The rest of us listen quietly at a deep level. Sometimes the inputs build into a theme and sometimes they don't. Often what is shared is only what can be shared with people where there is profound trust and confidentiality. We are frequently reminded of our mortality and fragility and of the perfection in our imperfection. We also remember group members who can't be with us. The ceremony concludes with a final meditation.

This may seem very simple, and it is. But attendees frequently comment on the sense of peace and fellowship that "Into Sacred Space" provides. For me it is a great example of the sort of local practice that men, women or mixed groups can adapt, adopt and experience. Any facilitated journey to inner peace has to have ripples in our wider lives. Who knows how this practice might enable greater wisdom for its participants in their subsequent and perhaps challenging encounters. Chris explains the origin of his group:

> Into Sacred Space came about when a small group of like-minded business friends started meeting following my experiences at a five-day Men's Rites of Passage in 2003. These Rites facilitated men to face their wounds, weakness, humiliations and mortality. The "Into" in the title of "Into Sacred Space" is important, signifying a movement from "business as usual" into a different space or level of consciousness when we meet. That said, we are beginning to fleetingly glimpse that maybe we are always in the peace and unity of Sacred Space if we can but recognise it.

Since writing this personal encounter, Chris Burford broke his neck in a skiing accident. I wish him and his family love for his recovery and the brightest possible future.

The freedom of peace   **53**

Logs in the fire

> Logs in the fire
> Burning brightly as one
> Separate them and the flame is gone
> Add another log and the fire burns bright
> Add too many and it just ain't right
> Congested, the flames have no room to breathe
>
> Without air there is no power
> And the flame dies by the hour
>
> And the first log
> The one that was there at the start
> The one who provided heart
> For initiation
> The one who created the situation
> Lies as ash in the grate
> And the fire burns on[12]

From local to global, we get to choose how we make an impact. There is no wrong or right in this. We take action as we are called and my next encounter is with a man who is having a global impact and deserves to have even more. I encourage you to check his work out, read his books and promote his thinking to any connections you may have, especially in government.

PERSONAL ENCOUNTER 2.4 – VIJAY MEHTA: "UNITING FOR PEACE"

I met Vijay Mehta[13] at the 2018 Uniting for Peace Spring Conference in London. I had been invited to speak to answer the question "Can We Unite for Peace: Building Citizen Power for Change".[14]

Vijay's book *Peace Beyond Borders: How the EU brought peace to Europe and how exporting it would end conflicts around the world* was published in 2016 in print and eBook by New Internationalist, with a foreword written by Jose Ramos-Horta, Nobel Peace Laureate and former president of Timor-Leste.

54 What is *beyond* sustainability? The six aspirations

I was inspired by Vijay's passion for the European Union model as mechanism for a more peaceful world. Conscious that since then we have witnessed a global pandemic, Brexit and the war in Ukraine, I was keen to catch up with him again.

In researching *Leading Beyond Sustainability*, I contacted Vijay in July 2023, and he kindly sent me a copy of his new book *How Not to Go to War – Establishing Departments for Peace and Peace Centres Worldwide*. In a similar fashion to *Peace Beyond Borders*, I found Vijay's thinking in this new book clear and compelling. I was unable to put it down! Vijay sets out the context for the proposition for such departments and centres with great clarity, explaining why things are as they are in a rational unemotional manner. His suggestions are logical and convincing, leaving me to wonder why there are not more such functions throughout the world.

His thinking is very much in line with my own. If we focus on the problem (e.g. war), our energy for change is limited. Whereas, if we focus on the opposite (peace), our creativity becomes boundless. Reading Vijay's book prompted many creative ideas in my own mind, including a need to revisit some of the other "personal encounters" featured in this chapter.

Vijay provided me with the best reason for hope at a most disturbing time in our history. His book was published in 2019, just before Russia's invasion of Ukraine in February 2022 which started a bloody war that would see hundreds of thousands of deaths, mainly of the young men (and fewer women) fighting on both sides of the conflict. The concept of investing in departments and centres for peace is so compelling that I can see very little argument against it. And, whilst no one wants to see war of any kind, maybe the colossal associated risk will shake the world into examining this and other potential solutions.

Later in July, I had the privilege of speaking with Vijay again. He recorded our conversation, and I added the video to the *Leading Beyond Sustainability* playlist on my YouTube channel. His passion for peace is immense.

If there had to be one single action that had the best chance to bring peace, it would be the creation of "Departments for Peace" in every government. The cost, in comparison to spending on war, would be tiny, and I fail to see how this wouldn't reduce the cost of conflict over time. And, I do mean every government: local, national and regional, with access to a growing number of professional "peace practitioners" who have studied the causes of peace and are keen to promote them. Duties would include (but not be limited to)

- Promoting constructive dialogue between nations and people of different cultures
- Monitoring potential areas of conflict and intervening before they flare up
- Encouraging inter-cultural and interfaith exchange
- Providing constructive activities, especially for young men, as alternatives to "street" violence
- Noticing, encouraging and celebrating peaceful initiatives
- Mediating in situations where conflict arises despite the above activities

I was delighted that, following my recent catch up with Vijay, he invited me once again to speak on the subject of *Leading Beyond Sustainability* at another of his powerful conferences. A recording of this conference is available on my YouTube channel.

Vijay's story is one of explicit and obvious peacemaking. I have also come to realise that there are many careers that have peacemaking deliberately woven into them. This is particularly the case in parts of the world where inter-cultural harmony has scope to be improved.

PERSONAL ENCOUNTER 2.5 – MARC JESSEL: "INTER-CULTURAL HARMONY"

In 2008, I was speaking at an HR Conference in Malawi which subsequently led to my first meeting with Marc Jessel[15] who was then Country Director for the British Council in Malawi. From the first time I met Marc, I could tell that he had a passion for peace and specifically for bringing people from different cultures together to learn, to share stories and to grow closer. Consequent to our meeting, and thanks to Marc, I had the joy of "going on tour" with my new colleague Christophe Horvath (introduced to me by Marc) to run a

56 What is *beyond* sustainability? The six aspirations

series of British Council "Talent Liberation" workshops in Southern Africa (Malawi, Mozambique, Zambia, Zimbabwe and Botswana). Then in 2009, Marc asked us to repeat the exercise in Jordan, Mauritius and Lebanon.

Christophe and I got to engage with hundreds of people to share insights on the value of understanding and playing to personal strengths in their lives and in their work. Most of all, it gave people the chance to get to know and encourage each other at a pretty deep level.

Marc and I kept in touch and, in 2022 he contacted me in his new role as Chief System Integrity Officer for the Forest Stewardship Council. As ever, Marc was keen to build bridges between people in the interests of making the world a better place, and my colleagues and I facilitated workshops for his team and in 2023 with another team from FSC. We also began to discuss other opportunities to enable better understanding and harmony within international organisations.

As I began writing this chapter on the aspiration of peace, I was reminded of Marc. I became more and more curious about what it was that motivated him in his work and whether there was any connection to his practice of Yoga. I asked him if he would be happy to explore this in a video interview.

Marc explained that there is more "peacemaking" built into the work of FSC than simply working with inter-cultural differences, powerful though this is. His organisation also works carefully to harmonise the interests of a diverse set of stakeholders and members who approach the topic of forests from very different perspectives (Economic, Social, Environmental, Global North, Global South). FSC acts as a convener and seeks to broker agreement between these different interests on how best to approach forest stewardship.

Of course, as well as FSC's less obvious work to build peace, the organisation also does an amazing job of delivering vitality through climate mitigation, habitat and leisure pursuits.

Another insight for me, consequent to my writing, is the extent that peacemaking often isn't labelled as such. A good example is in the corporate world, especially in global businesses where their expansion has taken them to new territories. Many businesses learn the hard way that the behaviours of their leaders don't work in other places. It has now become best practice to measure and manage the culture of any organisation and, where an organisation operates across global regions, to measure leadership characteristics that could potentially cause unhelpful and uncomfortable relationships.

PERSONAL ENCOUNTER 2.6 – OWEN WIBBERLEY AND JESSE ROWELL: "BEING *GLOBESMART*"

Owen Wibberley joined the Primeast[16] team of practitioners in 2020 when he returned to his native UK, having lived and worked in South Korea for about a decade. He arrived with his Korean wife and their two daughters and moved to Harrogate. I have had the privilege to facilitate alongside Owen and to hear his wisdom on a range of topics, including Diversity and Inclusion where he speaks convincingly from his studies and direct experience. He's also studying for a Masters in Global Cultures at Kings College, London, which is adding even more profound depth to his knowledge.

It is bizarre that it took my reading of Vijay Mehta's book *How Not to Go to War*, mentioned above, to make the link between Owen's work and our aspiration for global peace. We were working together at the Primeast office, scoping an intervention for one of my clients, focussing on smarter and more productive international working. We considered a range of tools that we thought would be useful to our client and opted for "Globesmart", as offered by Aperian, a US-headquartered consultancy that Primeast has partnered with for close to 20 years.

I had met Aperian's Managing Director, Global Mobility & Market Development, Jesse Rowell[17] when I was on a speaking trip to Texas in 2012, and I was well aware of the power of the Globesmart diagnostics to facilitate inter-cultural understanding and more harmonious and productive working. Yet, somehow, in my 20 years with Primeast, I had never fully considered its importance and impact on humanity's journey to world peace.

Working with Owen and reconnecting with Jesse during the same month as reading Vijay's book gave me a lightbulb moment that, once learned, I shall never forget. The connection is not just to Globesmart, powerful though this is, but also to the army of growing people-professionals now specialising in Diversity and Inclusion (in its many

58 What is *beyond* sustainability? The six aspirations

guises) who are consciously or unconsciously making significant contributions to world peace.

I thought it would be good to catch up with Owen and Jesse on a brief video call to explore the extent they had previously made such connections between their work and a more peaceful world.

We got to do this online in September 2023 and had a fabulous (recorded) conversation, now available on my YouTube channel in the *Leading Beyond Sustainability* playlist. We talked about the importance of people from all walks of life taking time to get to know each other and appreciate their different ways and cultural norms. We spoke just a few days after the G20 Summit and agreed that it must be really difficult for leaders to enter into such high-stakes dialogue without first having the opportunity to really get to know each other first. Jesse pointed out that, in our high-paced world, it might always seem to be too time consuming to collect informative data that would support productive dialogue. He also talked about the practicality of doing the same in business and pointed out how mergers and acquisitions are more prone to failure if the associated leaders fail to do the homework.

I think we all agreed that the world would definitely be a more peaceful place if people consciously took time to really understand each other before making assumptions or pushing their own agendas at the expense of others.

Chapter summary

Who are the individuals or organisations you know of who are actively promoting peace in our world – at any level?

Make a note of your top six (notice), preferably those where you have some kind of personal connection. Check them out online and post a suitable case study of your own on social media (celebrate) with your own words of encouragement. If you're struggling (which I doubt very much) then check out some of the cases in this chapter and simply post their work online.

And what about you? Make a note of six things you're already doing to promote peace. Then make a note of six more things you'd like to do in the future – preferably in your diary on the date you're going to make a start.

Notes

1 Wilson, C. A. 2023. The poem "Peace" by Author.
2 Our World in Data, 2024. Our World in Data: https://ourworldindata.org/
3 Pinker, S. 2024. Steven Pinker's books: https://stevenpinker.com/
4 United Nations, 2024. United Nations Sustainable Development Goals (SDGs): https://sdgs.un.org/goals
5 Wilson, C. A. 2018. *Designing the Purposeful World* by Clive Wilson: www.routledge.com/Designing-the-Purposeful-World-The-Sustainable-Development-Goals-as-a-Blueprint/Wilson/p/book/9780815381327
6 Vision of Humanity, 2024. Global Peace Index: www.visionofhumanity.org/
7 Institute for Economics & Peace, 2024. Institute for Economics and Peace: www.economicsandpeace.org/
8 Wikipedia, 2024. Vedran Smailovi: https://en.wikipedia.org/wiki/Vedran_Smailovi%C4%87
9 Resurgence & Ecologist, 2024. Satish Kumar: www.resurgence.org/satish-kumar/
10 Playing for Change, 2024. Playing for Change: www.playingforchange.com/
11 Wilson, 2023. Helen Wilson – playlist: https://youtube.com/playlist?list=PLBmmxnaj_ig_EhXzRnXSrXUScmocrDSsm&si=VSaUcbTjabv1Od_x
12 Wilson, C. A. 2022. The poem "Logs on the Fire" by Author.
13 Peace Building, 2024. Vijay Mehta: https://thepeacebuilding.org.uk/vijay-mehta/
14 Mehta, V. 2018. Clive's talk at Uniting for Peace (video): https://youtu.be/g3_747zs05s
15 Forest Stewardship Council International, 2024. Marc Jessel: https://fsc.org/en/leadership or LinkedIn
16 Primeast Ltd, 2024. Primeast: https://primeast.com/
17 Aperian, 2024. Aperian: https://aperian.com/

The joy of vitality 3

Vitality

The whole world breathes
The forest breathes out
And we breathe in
The wind howls up the valley
And swirls on the mountain crest

How fantastic that life simply happens
The design is built in
So we can run like the wind
Sleep like a baby
And fathom our greatest challenge

How wonderful this feeling of life
Playing out like a miracle

How privileged
To be tasked with design
Within our grasp
To bring vitality to all of life
By simply correcting what doesn't work
And facilitating what does

Let's face it
We can work with the miracle

DOI: 10.4324/9781003428121-5

The joy of vitality **61**

Or against it
But always the miracle prevails[1]

Vitality means much more than simply good health – it is about being fully alive and enjoying all that life offers us. It's also more than the health of humans. In this chapter, we also share perspectives on what it means to develop and live in a healthy world.

When we think of health, we might naturally think first about human health. However, we live in an interconnected world. We are part of an amazing ecosystem and, for us to thrive, the whole system must thrive. One aspect of this will be further expanded in the next chapter when we explore the aspiration of abundance and how we are growing our ability to provide nutritious food for a global population of around eight billion people and rising.

ACTIVITY

As in previous chapters, it's time to check out some of the masses of data that evidences progress to our own vitality and that of the wider world we live in. Revisit "Our World in Data" and look at the statistics such as how long people are living and how we have tackled ill health. Make your own notes in your journal.

By the way, you may well notice the severe adverse impact humans are having on indicators such as slaughtered animals, fish stocks and climate change. This may well fill you with despair. In this respect, I would also ask you to stay rational and check out trends around some of the new technologies that could rapidly reverse some of these adverse impacts. If you wish, you could check out the work of the RethinkX think tank (mentioned below in this chapter) to examine how technological disruption has the power to reverse some of humanity's adverse trends.

Incidentally, our global population is projected to reach over ten billion by the end of this century, largely due to a significant increase in life expectancy at birth. Globally, this reached 72.8 years in 2019, an increase of almost nine years since 1990. This encouraging data is one piece of evidence of improved human health. It is also perhaps encouraging to note that many predictions (including that of the UN median forecast) suggest our population will peak

62 What is *beyond* sustainability? The six aspirations

this century before we hit 11 billion and will then start to decline, arguably making it easier to manage our collective vitality. Some analysts suggest this is largely due to education, especially of women and girls, and the changing aspirations of young people in society.

The subject of vitality, well-being or good health is vast. So, this chapter barely scrapes the surface, sufficient to give us reassurance that vitality is improving rapidly with the potential of providing joy to all inhabitants, human or otherwise, of our precious world.

I'm going to start with a macro perspective and offer some thoughts and examples of amazing work being done to manage our climate and its impact on our lives. I shall then take a look at our planetary ecosystems before delving into the health of humanity. Finally, I shall offer some thoughts on personal health and well-being, including a taste of the complex industrial services that support our progress.

Climate change

Appropriately, a great deal of our focus right now is on the challenge of climate change. This has the potential to be catastrophic for humanity and many species. Yet, the more I examine what is being done to mitigate climate change, the more hopeful I become. The reasons for my hope lie in the vast breadth of work being done by so-called "ordinary people" and businesses on numerous fronts including the following:

Raising awareness about the impact of climate change

The speed at which growing numbers of people are awakening to the significant challenges posed by climate change is accelerating. This is due to a range of actors including education, journalism, social media, activism and also due to people directly experiencing the evidence of a changing climate firsthand. According to the Pew Research Centre, 67% of Americans perceived a rise in extreme weather in 2019,[2] even though opinions on the need for action seem to be divided, largely on party-political lines.

In Australia, according to national science, technology and environment reporter Michael Slezak in ABC News, the number of Australians believing that climate change[3] is actually occurring had increased by a staggering amount in just seven years. Around 20% believed this to be the case in 2013 compared to 80% in 2020.

The joy of vitality 63

We are investing significantly in climate-friendly technologies

From the now-famous Elon Musk at Tesla who has probably done more to electrify road transport than anyone on the planet, to the thousands of business leaders investing in a plethora of potentially game-changing technologies, we are already seeing major progress in the world of business.

The number of climate-friendly industries now in play is vast. They include forestry, rewilding, carbon trading, energy-reduction, renewable energy generation, nuclear fusion, ride-sharing, insulation, retrofit, permaculture, ocean recovery, climate-conscious agriculture and clean meat industries. This is just the tip of the iceberg. How many others can you think of?

Money follows the need

When well-respected economists such as past governor of the Bank of England, Mark Carney, talk about the emergence of a new age of business creating a better world and the death of what he called the "sunset sector" industries (e.g., fossil fuels)[4] and, similarly, the ex-CEO of Unilever, Paul Polman, co-authors with Andrew Winston a compelling book on *Net Positive: How Courageous Companies Thrive by Giving More Than They Take*,[5] the business economics shift quickly.

Sandra Haurant, in the *Guardian* newspaper, wrote on Tuesday 4 October 2022 the article *Green your pension: how you can help the environment*.[6] She suggests that from switching our investments to putting pressure on providers, we can help fight the climate crisis. Of course, before making any decisions about pensions and other investments, it is wise to take professional advice. You can find a list of independent financial advisers specialising in ethical investment on the Ethical Investment Association website.

Younger people entering the world of work are most likely to align with the climate opportunity

I use the word "opportunity" deliberately. Responding to climate change in a positive and creative manner is wise, necessary and a massive opportunity all at the same time. Check out *How climate change is re-shaping the*

64 What is *beyond* sustainability? The six aspirations

way Gen Z works by Christine Ro,[7] writing for *BBC Worklife* on 1 March 2022. Christine describes a high degree of climate anxiety amongst young people. However, this is also translating into positive intent and action. *This explosion of interest in values-related work is also reshaping the educational landscape. In the United States, increasing numbers of university students are seeking out environment-related careers, and there are ever more MBA programmes related to social impact and environment.*

I too discovered this when I began promoting the UN Sustainable Development Goals in 2015. As young people contemplated the prospect of a brighter future, many of them made the connection between this, what they cared about and what they were good at. One young man envisaged the oceans free from plastic and connected this vision to his love of marine biology and scuba diving – what an amazing career awaits him.

Examining the evidence

This future of humanity collaborating and co-operating to create a climate-friendly world is very much in play, and progress is accelerating. If you are in any doubt about this, please do your own research. An encouraging place to start is the work of Tony Seba and his colleagues at the RethinkX think tank in the United States. The report *Rethinking Humanity – Five Foundational Sector Disruptions, the Lifecycle of Civilizations, and the Coming Age of Freedom*[8] of June 2020 by James Arbib and Tony Seba is free to download at the RethinkX website and provides staggering evidence of the significant progress associated with innovative disruption in materials, food, energy, transport and information. Tony Seba also has a very accessible YouTube channel[9] for those preferring well-produced videos in bite-sized chunks.

A fairly recent addition to the RethinkX YouTube channel is a series of powerful videos by another RethinkX professional, Adam Dorr.[10] I have to say that I found the work of Dorr inspiring and thought-provoking. He builds on the data and trends offered by his colleagues above, adds in recent thinking about artificial intelligence and its effect on labour and the case for looking to new technological "tools" (as he calls them) becomes compelling. Dorr also sets out his case for turning to these tools in a wonderful book "Brighter", which I read in about a week as I couldn't put it down. Even the title of the book had a massive impact on my thinking – to the extent that I noticed how I automatically started replacing "better" with "brighter" throughout this book.

Indeed, my own 20-year-old definition of Purposeful Leadership, which was *consciously creating the conditions for a better future*, has now evolved into *consciously creating the conditions for a BRIGHTER future*. Thank you Adam!

I'd like to offer just a few case studies of my own to inspire you, the reader. Once more, this is not because I consider them to be the most powerful case studies in the field of climate management but because they are either unusual, come from my personal experience or a combination of the two.

The truth is, the more we open our eyes to what is happening in the world, the more we see. At this point, I will plug (again) my personal mantra:

> *Every time we notice, encourage and celebrate someone who is changing the world, we are changing the world*

It sounds too good to be true and so simple, but sharing news of someone doing something amazing, with someone else, is spreading inspiration and hope. Who knows what ripples of change we create? We can effect change in a conversation over a beer or by reposting good-news stories on social media. It all really helps.

Case studies from our oceans

In December 2022, BBC News published an article *How Seychelles ocean plants could help tackle climate change*.[11] The following brief extract captures the essence:

> Coastal wetlands – like seagrasses, mangroves, marshes and swamps – have multiple environmental benefits. As well as defending against rising waters and harsh weather caused by climate change, and promoting biodiversity, they are seen as one of the most effective solutions in fighting against global warming.

A study published in the Royal Society's flagship biological research journal says seagrasses capture carbon at a rate 35 times quicker than rainforests.[12] If undisturbed, they can hold carbon for thousands of years, far longer than terrestrial plants. They thereby play the role of a natural carbon sink.

66 What is *beyond* sustainability? The six aspirations

They account for 10% of the ocean's total burial of carbon, despite covering less than 0.2% of the ocean floor, a report in the scientific journal *Nature Geoscience* said.

Hold that thought.

When we think of capturing the excesses of carbon dioxide in our atmosphere many of us, quite understandably, will turn our minds to the vast forests that once covered our planet and still do provide massive opportunity as one piece of the climate challenge jigsaw.

But oceans and land at the water's edge also provide massive opportunity. Bill Adams is CEO of Leadership Circle,[13] an organisation committed to the promotion of "creative leadership". Bill is a man who truly "walks the talk". He is involved in climate mitigation through the preservation and development of mangrove swamps. This is a topic we discussed on a catchup call in 2022.

PERSONAL ENCOUNTER 3.1 – LUKE BIGWOOD: "THE ENVIRONMENT BANK"

I first met Luke when he was Head of Communications at Good Energy, a supplier of renewable energy in the UK. I had been to the firm in Chippenham to engage staff at a workshop on the United Nations Sustainable Development Goals. Luke and I had several enthusiastic conversations about sustainability, especially renewable energy and climate change. In 2017, Luke left Good Energy to become Head of Marketing and Communications at Yeo Valley, the UK's biggest organic brand, but returned to Good Energy at the beginning of 2020 as Marketing and External Affairs Director.

In the summer of 2023, I read with interest that Luke had been appointed as Chief Marketing Officer at Environment Bank.[14] Knowing his passion for sustainability, I wanted to know more about the company and Luke's new role.

Under the Environment Act 2021, all developments in England must deliver a minimum of 10% uplift in biodiversity to meet planning requirements. This is achieved through the creation and trade in "Biodiversity Net Gain" or BNG units.

To enable developers to meet their obligations under the Act, Environment Bank is establishing a network of "Habitat Banks" across the UK, at least one in each Local Planning Authority (LPA) to raise

BNG units. Strategically placed to create the best possible outcomes for nature – adjacent to pre-existing wildlife corridors and critical ecological networks – their Habitat Banks comprise a mosaic of high-quality habitats including species-rich meadows, woodlands and wetlands, all designed to restore and protect nature for generations to come.

This idea inspired me greatly, especially knowing, through the work of RethinkX (mentioned elsewhere in this book), that considerable land areas would soon be released from pasture as meat and other animal products from precision fermentation become cheaper and draw demand away from slaughterhouses.

BNG units are an innovative way to unlock economic growth, improve nature, and provide developers with a simple, risk-free way to implement BNG. The units are fully compliant with national and local planning policies and are compatible with both section 106 agreements and conservation covenants. They provide an auditable and robust solution, helping LPAs meet their obligations as set out in the Environment Act and achieve the UK Government's Net Zero ambitions by 2050.

The Environment Bank's unique selling point is straightforward. It makes implementing BNG simple by joining the dots between developers and planning authorities. It removes the burden and the risks from developers, whilst fully supporting the planning process and providing a seamless service to LPAs for the life of the BNG commitment.

And, just to demonstrate the extent of the amazing oceanic innovation in play right now, here is something completely different.

PERSONAL ENCOUNTER 3.2 – HEATH JACKSON: "HAVE YOU EVER HEARD OF *LIGHT TREES*?"

Just before the Covid-19 pandemic, I spent a great deal of my time coaching some of the senior partners at global consulting firm KPMG. One of the leaders I spent time with was Heath Jackson[15] (who kindly

68 What is *beyond* sustainability? The six aspirations

also wrote the foreword to this book). Heath had this to say about the time we spent together:

> Successful coaching is all about the chemistry between coach and coachee. Trust and challenge in equal measures. Clive and I made a pretty instant connection, and he challenged my thinking from the start to tease out some thoughts that I probably hadn't verbalised even to myself. Whilst we absolutely completed the job at hand, our conversations quickly grew legs and got me thinking way out of the intended box!

Since then, Heath has truly followed his personal purpose to only support organisations that are making the world a better place. Since retiring from KPMG, he has made himself available as a non-executive director to such organisations, including Ecopia. I reference this work as an example of amazing work in hand that few readers will have heard about (at least at the time of writing) but which could make a massive contribution to the well-being of our planet.

Ecopia aims to "green the deep blue deserts of the oceans" (wow).
These deserts, to be precise, are Oligotrophic Gyres. They exist in each of the world's oceans, and the five major gyres take up one-seventh of the ocean's surface area. They are growing with time. These giant ocean circulations have a stable water column that locks nutrients below the thermocline (100–300-m deep) and currently contributes disproportionately little to overall ocean CO_2 uptake with respect to their surface area. They exist in International waters and are home to the sprawling ocean garbage patches.

The Ecopia strategy is to use light to "irrigate" the oceans.
The key technology is the use of light trees to pipe light (and heat) down to below the thermocline and access essentially unlimited nutrients. This process creates vertically stacked green fields of phytoplankton. The light can be regulated to control productivity and carbon uptake. Each light tree stimulates carbon uptake of around 50 kg of carbon per year. The process does not pollute the environment and ultimately decomposes to nutrients needed by the phytoplankton.

Ecopia will deploy numerous light trees to create "light forests" using a modular approach and scaling up in size. This allows for experimentation with different approaches to scaling and construction. Their work will be done in collaboration with the shipping, oil and maritime construction industries. It is intended that this massive global cooperation will achieve incredible outcomes.

Technology for construction exists today, it just needs scaling. Find out more about the amazing work of Ecopia at their website.[16]

Our precious ecosystem

I can't think of anyone who has done more in recent years to raise our awareness to the splendour and interconnection of life on our planet than Sir David Attenborough. Born on 8 May 1926 he is an English broadcaster, biologist, natural historian and author, best known for writing and presenting, in conjunction with the BBC Natural History Unit, the nine natural history documentary series forming the life collection, a comprehensive survey of animal and plant life on earth.[17]

Sir David has inspired a generation of eco-enthusiasts, myself included. You will probably be very familiar with his work. What you might not know is that, amongst the many people he has inspired, is Sue Flood, a Wrexham-based wildlife photographer. Sue spoke of her time with David Attenborough and how people can be more environmentally friendly just ahead of the release of her book *Emperor – The Perfect Penguin* in 2018.[18] Sue made an ambitious intention and subsequently worked with Sir David as an associate producer on television series such as *The Blue Planet* and *Planet Earth*.

Sue's book is a celebration of one of the world's most charismatic creatures. In temperatures that can reach $-50°C$ with 150 km/h winds, the emperor penguins' ability to survive and thrive is nothing short of astounding. As an award-winning photographer, Sue has journeyed to remote Antarctic penguin colonies to capture the birds in their native home.

Sue Flood's respect for her subjects emanates from every page. From the poignant sight of an egg abandoned on the sea ice to majestic shots of emperor penguins returning from the sea and heart-warming photos of chicks clustering together for warmth, every shot explores a new angle of life in this remote and ice-crusted world.

Contemplating Sue Flood's impact through imagery and storytelling makes me think of the millions of artists, teachers, writers and other

70 What is *beyond* sustainability? The six aspirations

enthusiasts who serve to accelerate progress to our brighter future through their natural ability to inspire. And sometimes inspiration comes from visiting a beautiful place and forming a desire to see more of the same. This is definitely the case for my next encounter.

PERSONAL ENCOUNTER 3.3 – DAN CARNE: "THE JOY OF WOODMEADOWS"

As my world began to open up after the Covid-19 pandemic, one of the first face-to-face workshops I ran was in the beautiful setting of the Three Hagges Woodmeadow at Escrick near York, run by the Woodmeadow Trust. This is just a few miles from my home in North Yorkshire, UK. I had previously met Dan Carne, Director of the UK Woodmeadow Network, through my work as chair of our local United Nations Association branch and was impressed by his knowledge and enthusiasm about woodmeadows and the habitats they provide to an incredible ecosystem.

Dan told me about the Three Hagges Woodmeadow run by the Trust and providing a fabulous outdoor venue for workshops and education. In this one site alone, the Trust made a significant impact in reversing a dramatic decline in wildlife by creating a gorgeous woodmeadow at this flagship site.

I had a workshop I needed to run for Energy Oasis, a local business involved in climate mitigation through energy monitoring, energy management and renewable generation. The 25-acre woodmeadow with its pathways and various rustic meeting shelters was perfect for our workshop, and our attendees learnt not only about climate mitigation from Energy Oasis but also a great deal about the power of ecosystems from Dan and the Woodmeadow Trust team. In 2023, Woodmeadow Trust was assimilated into Plantlife International,[19] a global charity working to enhance, protect, restore and celebrate the wild plants and fungi that are essential to all life on earth. In the UK, Plantlife is particularly well known for its work on wildflower meadow restoration and the "No Mow May" campaign. Three Hagges Woodmeadow is now one of their 24 nature reserves in the UK, and it continues to be managed for wildlife with the help of a dedicated team of volunteers.

The joy of vitality **71**

Dan's enthusiasm for conservation is infectious. He had this to say about his work:

Woodmeadows are spectacular habitats that have largely disappeared in Britain due to agricultural intensification. Grasslands with scattered trees, managed as hay meadows, these systems have been widespread across Europe for more than 4,000 years. Historically, lots of our orchards, churchyards, parklands and woodlands were used to graze livestock and produce animal fodder, timber, fruit and nuts. Woodmeadows aren't "wild", they're the result of human intervention – and that's part of why I love them. Despite their human origins, woodmeadows are amongst the most biodiverse habitats in the world. One Estonian woodmeadow holds the European record for small-scale diversity, with 76 plant species found in a single square metre of ground. That's more than you'd find in a square metre of tropical rainforest!

The global nature of the climate and biodiversity crisis is intimidating, and lots of us question the difference that we can make as individuals. However, in my work I get to work with lots of community groups, private landowners and local councils, and have visited hundreds of extraordinary projects that are having a profoundly positive impact on both wildlife and people. These projects vary massively in size. One is a 300-acre woodmeadow at the edge of Reading incorporating more than 50,000 trees and a wetland that will help to alleviate local flooding. At the opposite extreme is a playing field I visited last week in Yorkshire with a woodmeadow in the corner that covers less than a quarter of an acre, but nevertheless provides a secluded oasis for local people. Volunteers have grown and planted hundreds of wildflowers, with help from local schoolchildren.

Sometimes in our rush to reduce our carbon footprint, we forget that trees, grassland and other habitats can do more for us than just lock up carbon. Trees help to improve air quality, reduce temperatures in urban areas and provide shade and shelter for livestock. Green spaces can also have a powerful impact on our mental and physical well-being. Open spaces and woodland edge habitats are particularly important for wildlife, and these areas can act as biodiversity hotspots whilst also providing a welcoming sunny environment for people to enjoy.

72 What is *beyond* sustainability? The six aspirations

My personal encounters above have focused on environmental issues, looking at just a few of the heroes at work making our planet a healthier place for all of life. I'd like to zoom in now to the challenge of maintaining healthy communities of people in the UK. So it would be remiss not to feature the amazing work of our health service here in the UK. My next three encounters all impact the effectiveness of the health service but in very different ways. I hope this demonstrates the complexity that has grown in society to keep us all alive and well.

PERSONAL ENCOUNTER 3.4 – CARA CHARLES-BARKS AND ALFREDO THOMPSON: "CULTURAL HEALTH OF A HEALTH PROVIDER"

Cara Charles-Barks is CEO of Royal United Hospitals Bath National Health Service Trust[20] and Alfredo Thompson is Director of People and Culture.

I had the pleasure of meeting Cara and Alfredo in 2022 when Primeast was asked to support them in a program to launch a new Trust strategy and improve the organisation's culture.

The Executive Team had spent the previous 24 months leading an organisation that was at the centre of the local Covid-19 response. Consequently, the team was experiencing fatigue and had received feedback from the Senior Leadership team that there was a need for greater clarity in priorities and direction. We agreed to support the alignment of the whole leadership community behind this new direction and bring it to life, thus creating the conditions for a better future.

Together with the leadership team, we agreed to establish a "leadership heart" for the Trust which would initially be vested in the top 43 leaders and would align the strategy, values and behaviours. It was critical that the values-based approach should be lived out every day in the observable behaviours of senior leaders.

Just as it is important to diagnose any (medical) health condition before prescribing treatment, so it is important to diagnose corporate (cultural) health before working with leaders to adopt new behaviours and deliver cultural transformation. We therefore agreed with the leadership team to measure the current and intended cultures using the method offered by Barrett Values Centre. This is a best-in-class method for diagnosis that Alfredo was also very familiar with and accredited in.

The survey identified a desire amongst leaders to establish a progressive culture comprising the following:

- Compassionate leadership
- Continuous Improvement
- Greater accountability
- Blame-free operation
- High-performing teamwork
- Innovation
- Greater empowerment
- Leading by example
- A longer-term perspective
- Shared vision

Senior leaders also received coaching from me on how to deliver this, taking account of their own personal values. We worked together to identify practical actions that each leader could deliver and share progress together as a team.

A year on from this intervention, Cara commented on the progress that has been made:

We are making slow and steady progress. The most important thing for us is to create hope and momentum around the future we want to create for both our staff and the people we care for. We are trying to achieve this in an external landscape that is becoming increasingly complicated as we see the impact of the wider economic challenges, global issues and increasing pressure in health service delivery. Understandably our journey is bumpy as creating the change we want requires energy, commitment and tenacity from everyone in the organisation. We are harnessing the positive energy and supporting those teams that are finding the changes harder – for us it is always keeping our people and our values central to what we do. If we don't keep a strong focus on the people we work with we won't be able to achieve the excellence we aspire to for the people we care for and our wider community.

74 What is *beyond* sustainability? The six aspirations

The wider (but still explicit) health system

I'd like to move gently outwards from the core of our health service to the environment presented by the communities we live in. I also sense a strong link here to our second aspiration, that of peace. I'm not the only one thinking this way. There are countless people all over the world helping to make communities become more peaceful, more harmonious and more conducive to meaningful and healthy lives. I'm fortunate to have had the opportunity to meet, get to know and listen to one of them.

PERSONAL ENCOUNTER 3.5 – MATT WALSH: "COMMUNITIES OF WELL-BEING"

One thing that really stuck in my mind from my studies for my MSc in Safety and Reliability in the 1990s was watching my professor, Dr Alfred Z Keller, scribe a formula on the blackboard in good old-fashioned chalk. "Do you know what this means, Clive?" he asked. I confessed that I had no idea, and he explained that anything invested in maintenance will save us at least ten times that amount in repair. Since then, I have appreciated that this applies to just about anything in life: machinery, buildings, roads, climate and even health. With this in mind, I have often wondered what vast savings could be achieved in the work of health services if more was spent on the well-being of communities. Savings, that is, in terms of money and ill health.

Just as the global pandemic was forcing populations all around the world into lockdown, I was introduced by a mutual friend to Doctor Matt Walsh,[21] previously a Health Service Chief Executive, who had started a consultancy aimed at helping the disparate organisations involved in delivering health and well-being to work together in promoting vitality in communities and thereby reducing the burden on the UK National Health Service. One of Matt's projects has been to support the work of Bradford District and Craven healthcare partnership, a partnership of statutory and non-statutory organisations working to the declared ambition of keeping people "happy, healthy at home".

The focus is on preventing ill health as much as possible by creating opportunities that help people stay healthy, well and independent and tackle inequalities across communities. Priorities include prioritising prevention and early intervention, fostering healthy lifestyles, self-care and nurturing active communities so that people are happier, healthier and more independent.

When people need care and support from these services, they become easy to access, joined up, designed around their needs and provided as close to where they live as possible.

The aim is for people to be healthier, happier and have access to high-quality care that is clinically, operationally and financially stable. In other words, people will be as safe as possible when accessing care whilst ensuring the best use is made of the resources funded by taxpayers. Not just that, but communities and professionals get to work together in the creation of happier and healthier communities.

Matt is an experienced coach, mentor, facilitator, and leadership development practitioner collaborating with clients from a range of settings and levels of seniority within and outside health and care. He is a former General Practitioner and senior National Health Service (NHS) leader; he now works within the field of leadership and has extensive experience in organisational and systems development. Matt's approach is to establish safe developmental spaces for those who are responsible for leading organisations and systems. With a keen interest in the relationship between humanity, creativity and well-being, in his role as co-chair of The Creative Health and Wellbeing Alliance, he convenes environments where creative people from the worlds of health and the arts can meet and work together. He also provides strategic advice to those working to develop their thinking about systems working and the role of primary care.

Here Matt describes an example of where this has worked well and which we can all relate to:

> After spending most of my professional lifetime completely committed to improvement and to the reduction of inequalities in health that I encountered along the way, I realised that rather than things getting better, things had in fact, in many ways, got worse. My first response to this insight was that this fact was itself a demonstration of my complete lack of impact and my extraordinary incompetence during my time as a doctor in general practice.

Some, I am sure, would agree. But stepping away from a role in which I had accountability for work to address quality in inequality, I can see now, and I suppose always knew, that the drivers for these perennial challenges are many and complex. As I get older, I understand better that relationship is at the heart of everything. Love is what first drives improvement, and it will be love that wakes the world up to the need to address inequality.

It was with this knowledge in my heart that I embarked on a project with colleagues in the Bradford, Airedale and Craven (BAC) district in 2020 to establish an approach to what is known as Population Health Management (PHM). PHM is an attempt to identify within populations, those groups of people who are at greatest risk from disease, on the basis of better analysis of data that the health and care system has already gathered within the process of caring for people at an individual level.

We know, because the evidence tells us, that if we more proactively identify and manage risk then we can reduce the impact that disease can have and we can increase the number of years that people can live without being dependent upon medicines, others or the state. That is a "good thing", though I would be the first to agree that thinking like this already is too heavily invested in a medical model; happiness, joy and fulfilment are about so much more than the absence of disease, and their presence in our lives is dependent upon so much more than "the identification and management of clinical risk".

In bringing people together, we convene a space between those working within organisations, enabling a conversation about priorities, about how we will work together, about how we will share information and share our resources in support of a shared endeavour to improve the lives of the citizens we are here to serve. We are able to agree on how we will do that with people and not do it to them. We are able to go where the energy and momentum are, settling on the one priority that everyone could agree upon – the better identification of those in the earliest stages of diabetes – where the district is recognised nationally as an outlier and has been for decades.

Our series of conversations turned ideas into a clear set of priorities, actions, specific populations to focus upon first and ultimately a strategy, with a senior-level steering group to oversee the delivery.

The joy of vitality **77**

> Matt's story fills me with massive admiration for the army of people around the world who are supporting wellness in our communities, be they teachers, sports clubs, gymnasiums, scientists working on health diagnostics or simply enthusiastic people organising park-runs or a walk in the countryside with friends.

The infrastructure for vitality is complex and further reaching than it may at first seem. For every person who describes themselves as a health and care worker, including doctors, nurses, carers, anaesthetists, physiotherapists and so on, there are a hundred others who make similar impact but wouldn't usually receive their deserved credit from society – or even (or especially) from themselves.

PERSONAL ENCOUNTER 3.6 – TIM HOPKINSON: "LIFE-SAVING DUCTWORK"

It was 2016, and I was lying in a hospital bed with an immense feeling of gratitude. After a year or so of severe arthritis, probably self-inflicted from 27 years of playing far too much rugby, my hip required replacement. The operation had gone well, and I was able to eat a delicious hospital meal and take a look around.

From my bed, I began noticing and thinking about the complexity of our health service and the people who make it happen. The obvious candidates came to mind quickly: the surgeon, the anaesthetist, the nurses, the porters, the chef and so on. Then I thought of the engineers, builders, maintenance teams, the inventors and producers of medical equipment and pharmaceutical products. The list is endless.

The thing is this, when we think of people who work to save and improve lives in our health services, we tend to think of the obvious – until we really think.

I was reminded of a conversation I had had with the senior vice president of an organisation who wrote software for medical scanners. He was wondering how to retain his talented software engineers who were leaving for higher salaries elsewhere. I asked him how aware they were of the fact that their software actually saves lives. It was a lightbulb moment, and I trust the insight allowed this leader to inspire his people with the real purpose of their work. But that isn't the personal encounter I'd like to focus on.

I met Tim Hopkinson when he was managing director at an engineering company in the north of England. I had worked with him to build and align his senior leaders to their work. In 2023, Tim contacted me again asking me to repeat this work for his new business in North Wales.

Poppleton has been manufacturing and installing quality ventilation and air movement solutions since 1924. Today their systems operate at the heart of the health sector in hospitals and laboratories, as well as in other industries such as the nuclear power sector. These systems are essential to the efficient, safe and healthy conditions we absolutely rely on and which most of us take for granted.

I was with the Senior Leadership team at Poppleton[22] and listened intently as Tim and his co-director, Nigel Edwards-Hughes, described the importance of the company's work and mentioned the fact that next year would be the company's centenary.

I was then able to work with the senior team for two days. The primary purpose was to strengthen the team and their personal leadership capabilities. In the conversations we had, it was apparent that most of the employees at Poppleton would never think of their work as life saving. "We make ducts and install them" was the prevailing and down-to-earth story.

We covered a lot of ground during our two days together but the most inspiring outcome, certainly for me, was the intention of this team of leaders to take their 2024 centenary year and truly celebrate the importance of the company's work as an essential ingredient in the life-saving work of health and pharmaceutical industries as well as in other critical infrastructure projects.

The team has made plans to celebrate the centenary and the company's work internally with their workforce as well as externally with their customers and suppliers. They are in little doubt that this will be inspirational to all stakeholders as well as good for future business.

Poppleton is not alone in the tendency to focus on "what" gets done in workplaces around the world. Far more important is to ask the question "Why?".

For Tim Hopkinson, sharing this insight widely and encouraging others to do the same in their industries is key to delivering a better world for future generations:

> All too often, individuals and organisations focus upon delivering outcomes which have possibly been unchanged for many, many years. They can lose sight of the positive impact which they deliver, not just to their business but also to the wider community, the environment and to others. Aligning everyone to the same purpose and inspiring others to lead and innovate through empowerment is important not only to deliver good business but also to ensure that products and services constantly evolve. No one person has all of the answers but as professionals we have a moral and ethical obligation to encourage our team members to contribute and, in doing so, we will see benefit both for our business and the environment in which we all live.

When we stop and think about the complexity of providing a functional health service, we begin to take notice of the vast network of suppliers whose work helps the system work with ever-improving efficiency. My previous "encounter" was a good example of one industry that contributes to the infrastructure in hospitals and laboratories. My next one focuses on the movement of qualified people around the health service and other organisations.

PERSONAL ENCOUNTER 3.7 – RICHARD ETHERIDGE: "MOVING NURSES TO WHERE THEY'RE MOST NEEDED"

A very good friend and business associate, Paul Chubb, contacted me a couple of years ago, at the time of the Covid-19 pandemic. He told me about a company he was on the board of as a non-executive director. Axia Digital[23] has been helping organisations capture and assess skills and competencies that are demonstrated in a professional setting or in the workplace. They create digital solutions, which mirror and then enhance existing assessment systems. These solutions are all individually handcrafted but are deployed on the same platform.

80 What is *beyond* sustainability? The six aspirations

Paul asked me if I'd be happy to meet up with Axia's Managing Director, Richard Etheridge, who was seeking an executive coach. As this was during lockdown, Richard and I met online. We got on well and began a programme of executive coaching as well as the facilitation of his team of software developers to improve performance and meet the challenges of a changing world.

Over the course of our work together, Richard told me a great deal about the amazing work of his company. He was particularly proud of the work they had done to develop digital passports, a continuing area of growth for the business.

Skills passports allow staff to demonstrate their core skills effectively and easily against a standardised framework and share this information quickly with fellow professionals and line managers across their organisation. This enables staff to move across locations without the need for lengthy skills checking and assessment procedures, saving time and money for employers and organisations.

One such project inspired me greatly and (as in my previous encounter) increased my sense of gratitude for the variety of businesses working together to ensure healthcare is provided as efficiently as possible.

Critical Care Passports create a mobile workforce and were first developed in response to a request from The Imperial College Health Care Trust during the second wave of the Covid-19 pandemic in London. Axia worked with the team in record time to develop the Critical Care Passport, which enabled medical staff to move across the capital's Intensive Care Units and get straight to work saving lives.

The passport in this case contained all the required capabilities and information about equipment the individual was trained to use, in an easily accessible format. When a staff member arrived at a new ward, a skills-checking process that would previously have taken a number of hours was greatly reduced. It also provided invaluable information for line managers who could familiarise themselves with the skills and knowledge of incoming staff before shifts started and plan how to utilise team members effectively.

Jane Fish the project manager explained the purpose of the PAN London Critical Care Passport:

> This work led by Clare Leon Villapalos, (Imperial College Health Care Trust) in partnership with stakeholders across London, on the CC Skills Passport for Registered Support Clinician (RSC) and Non-Registered Support Staff (NRSS) roles will make an important

contribution to preparing and supporting staff redeployed during surge to ICU and Covid clinical areas. Providing the Skills Passport on a digital platform will enhance its accessibility for both RSC and NRSS users as well as for the staff working in the environments where staff members have been redeployed.

Following the success in London, the Critical Skills Passport has been rolled out across England.

Richard had this to say about the scope of this kind of work into the future:

We have had many conversations with organisations over the last 18 months about passports and how they can support the workforce in ways that traditional HR systems cannot as we are focusing on capabilities which I consider outputs rather than traditional inputs such as training and learning. Being output-based we focus on the capabilities of the workforce in relation to delivery to the service user. Where this can start to get more interesting is when you aggregate these capabilities up through an organisation, as you start to map the skills within the workforce which in turn supports analysis for gaps and succession planning. The mapping of the skills can be taken further where you align capabilities across roles and allow further analysis of transferability within the workforce.

Chapter summary

Who are the individuals or organisations you know of who are actively promoting vitality and improving the well-being of humanity, all of life and the world we live in? These are the people helping us to be fully alive and enjoying all that life offers us.

Make a note of your top six (notice), preferably those where you have some kind of personal connection. Check them out online and post a suitable case study of your own on social media (celebrate) with your own words of encouragement. If you're struggling (which I doubt very much) then check out some of the cases in this chapter and simply post their work online.

And what about you? Make a note of six things you're already doing for your own vitality, for the well-being of others or for the health of our planet. Then make a note of six more things you'd like to do in the future – preferably in your diary on the date you're going to make a start.

82 What is *beyond* sustainability? The six aspirations

Notes

1 Wilson, C. A. 2024. Poem "Vitality" by Author.
2 Funk, C. & Tyson, A. 2021. Pew Research Centre: www.pewresearch.org/short-reads/2021/10/14/67-of-americans-perceive-a-rise-in-extreme-weather-but-partisans-differ-over-government-efforts-to-address-it/#:~:text=67%25%20of%20Americans%20perceive%20a,government%20efforts%20to%20address%20it&text=Two%2Dthirds%20of%20Americans%20say,often%20than%20in%20the%20past.
3 Slezak, M., 2020. ABC News: www.abc.net.au/news/2020-10-28/australia-institute-2020-climate-change-report-concern-growing/12764874
4 Carrington, D. 2019. The *Guardian*: www.theguardian.com/environment/2019/oct/13/firms-ignoring-climate-crisis-bankrupt-mark-carney-bank-england-governor
5 Polman, P. & Winston, A. 2021. *Net Positive*: https://hbr.org/2021/09/the-net-positive-manifesto
6 Haurant, S. 2022. The *Guardian*: www.theguardian.com/money/2022/oct/04/green-pension-help-environment-climate-crisis
7 Ro, C. 2022. BBC: www.bbc.com/worklife/article/20220225-how-climate-change-is-re-shaping-the-way-gen-z-works
8 RethinkX, 2024. RethinkX: www.rethinkx.com/humanity
9 Seba, T. 2024. Tony Seba: www.youtube.com/@tonyseba
10 RethinkX, 2024. Adam Dorr: https://youtube.com/playlist?list=PLxB143vg5_msNrYjoVRUv4IHphHf1Qmq_&si=nxZN2VoMtpCFDTEB
11 Buyoya, D. J. 2022. BBC: www.bbc.co.uk/news/world-africa-63901644
12 Macreadie, P. I., Trevathan-Tackett, S. M., Skilbeck, C. G., Sanderman, J., Curlevski, N., Jacobsen, G. & Seymour, J. R. 2015. Royal Society: https://royalsocietypublishing.org/doi/10.1098/rspb.2015.1537
13 Leadership Circle, 2024. Bill Adams, Leadership Circle: https://leadershipcircle.com/wp-content/uploads/2020/10/Adams-Bill-bio-MAY-2020.pdf
14 Environment Bank, 2024. Environment Bank: https://environmentbank.com/discover/our-team
15 Linked In, 2024. Heath Jackson: www.linkedin.com/in/heathsjackson/
16 Ecopia, 2024. Ecopia: https://ecopia.world/
17 Wikipedia, 2024. David Attenborough: https://en.wikipedia.org/wiki/David_Attenborough
18 Flood, S. 2011. Sue Flood: www.sueflood.com/shop/category/books/
19 Plantlife, 2024. Plantlife: www.plantlife.org.uk/
20 NHS Royal United Hospitals Bath, 2024. Royal United Hospitals: www.ruh.nhs.uk/
21 Linked In, 2024. Dr Matt Walsh: www.linkedin.com/in/matt-walsh-9a803927/
22 E Poppleton & Son Ltd, 2024. Poppleton: https://poppleton.co.uk/
23 Axia Digital, 2024. Axia Digital: www.axiadigital.uk/

A spirit of abundance 4

Abundance

What an amazing planet
With enough of everything for everyone
To live life and have fun

Food from the garden
And from the tall tower
Energy from the sun
To grow the flower
And light our streets
Whatever the hour

And from the wind and sea
How cool can that be

Clean water from the rivers
Even from the sea
To quench our thirst
And set us free

Metals and minerals
Used with care
To make cutlery and cars
To take us here and there
We need to be wise

DOI: 10.4324/9781003428121-6

84 What is *beyond* sustainability? The six aspirations

And not abuse this prize
Take no more than we need
No more than we should
And reuse what we have
Again and again

Just as water in the sky
Falls as rain
Again and again

And again[1]

The premise of this aspiration is that, with innovation and wisdom (see Chapter 6), our world offers an abundance of all the resources we need, including food, water, energy, services and wealth – "sufficient for everyone's need and no-one's greed" (E F Schumacher). As we learn how to manage and share resources, we also remove many of the drivers of conflict.

Over half a century has now passed since Ernst Schumacher wrote *Small Is Beautiful: A Study of Economics as if People Mattered* (1973).[2] Schumacher was Chief Economic Adviser to the UK National Coal Board from 1950 to 1970 and during this time, in 1955, he travelled to Burma as an economic consultant. Whilst he was there, he coined the term *Buddhist Economics*, introducing a set of principles based on the belief that individuals need good work for proper human development. Far from being some quirky activist, Schumacher also wrote on economics for *The Times* newspaper and became one of the paper's chief editorial writers.

The truth is apparent. We live on a very special planet with finite resources. However, with informed strategies, we have sufficient resources to feed the world, provide clean water and sanitation, generate abundant clean energy, travel just about anywhere without destroying our planet and create wealth which, in turn, offers opportunity for everyone to lead their best life.

The more I explore our world and meet its leaders, the more I see action on so many fronts to tap into and channel abundant food, water, energy, services and wealth. Millions of people are engaged in this work every single day. They are discovering new ways of doing things, improving the efficiency of our methods, eliminating waste and making resources available and affordable to everyone who needs them.

The decline of poverty

We have already made significant progress in terms of enabling people to climb away from poverty. We should remind ourselves that, in just 200 years, we have reduced the percentage of our global population living in extreme poverty from 79% to just 9%. Of course, that is no reason to rest on our laurels. One person living in poverty is one too many. There are still parts of the world where poverty is the norm and, even in wealthy countries such as Britain and the United States, we still find homeless people rough-sleeping and facing abject poverty. The key thing is that the trend is a good one.

ACTIVITY

You can check out the above statistics once again at "Our World in Data". In addition, take a look at other indicators of growth in abundance. Browse the data sufficiently to understand the complexity of our aspiration of abundance. Notice how easy it is to deplete the world's resources through over-consumption of certain products. Notice how inequality affects the viability of our brighter future. But also bear in mind and check out evidence that growth can happen without destroying our precious world. Perhaps take another look for clues at RethinkX. I'll say more below.

A critical balance

We are faced with quite a dilemma and an opportunity. On the one hand, it makes absolute sense not to waste precious resources or pollute our world through our actions. At the same time, it seems unfair to deny a good standard of living to everyone, especially if doing so can be achieved without harm to our planet.

We rapidly approach a time when abundant low-cost clean energy and low-cost labour through artificial intelligence and robotics will enable us to reach abundance without pollution. These factors will also enable us to use our new technologies to reverse harm that has been done in recent decades.

86 What is *beyond* sustainability? The six aspirations

Simultaneously, new food technologies such as clean meat and precision fermentation will free up masses of land, currently used for pasture, which can be put to good use and contribute to climate mitigation, habitat creation, leisure facilities and a host of other ecologically sound ventures. These developments also offer exciting new career paths for people new to the labour market or who have been displaced due to technological disruption.

The myth of scarcity

Considering all this, I'd like to pose a controversial question. I often hear and read environmental campaigners making statements such as "we can't have infinite growth on a finite planet". It's a good thought and one that I've tended to agree with for most of my life. But, as I've been researching this book, I'm beginning to see things differently. It all depends on how we see growth. Let me offer the following thought experiments:

1. Suppose we make a useful product using a fraction of the material required for the previous versions and can do so using materials recovered by recycling the old products. So, one widget is used to make four superior widgets at a fraction of the cost. Is this "growth" desirable? Is it progress? Is it adding value?
2. In a similar way, what if we can recover scarce minerals from old products and use them in a far more efficient way (such as by 3D printing) in new products, thus making better use of scarce materials? Is this growth and progress desirable or undesirable?
3. What if we devise intelligent systems (which cost money and would contribute to GDP) that minimise waste (e.g., food waste)? Would such industry be a good thing?
4. And, for something completely different, what if we take time and care to produce a wonderful painting using a fraction of the materials we might have used to produce ten lower-quality works of art and sell the painting for a hundred times the sum of that for the ten? Is this growth?
5. Look at advances in computing. We now have many times more computers in the world and a significant number the size of a mobile phone, which, by the way, also does the job of the camera and voice recorder we used to use, now in a box in the attic waiting to be recycled. Is this growth or not?
6. Did you once have a bookshelf full of video tapes? Do you now store them on a hard drive that is smaller than a single tape?

A spirit of abundance **87**

Can you think of other ways we have made a distinct growth in value whilst actually using less of the world's valuable resources? Maybe, therefore, an abundance and a growth mindset is feasible on a finite planet, if we approach growth with a degree of wisdom and creativity.

I hope you enjoy my personal encounters around the aspiration of abundance. These are all people and organisations that have been part of my life and whose achievements I am proud to celebrate. As with the other aspirations, the point is that there are millions of such people around the world, and some that you will know well, which is why we're making such good progress.

PERSONAL ENCOUNTER 4.1 – SUCHETA AND SHAIL JAIN: "ALIGNING PURPOSE TO THE EFFICIENT DELIVERY OF SERVICES TO COMMUNITIES"

This personal encounter is a wonderful example of a business contributing significantly to making the world a better place for communities, almost without realising the true impact of its work.

Over the past three decades, Farragut[3] has grown to become one of the leading workers' compensation and property tax solution providers in the United States.

In 2021, the business owners, Sucheta and Shail Jain, contacted me for personal consultancy to support the business on its journey of purpose and values. This is what Sucheta had to say about what she describes as the company's journey:

> The journey of purpose and values has been important to us since the beginning of Farragut's founding. We want this company to survive for 100 years or longer and continue serving our customers, employees and communities. We know that the only way for that longevity is to have a strong foundation. What better way to build a strong foundation for a long-living company than to have a well-defined purpose and a set of values? A question that we have asked ourselves is: why does Farragut exist? The answer to that question for us is:

Farragut exists to help:

- Our customers reach their full potential and help their customers reach their full potential.

88 What is *beyond* sustainability? The six aspirations

- Our employees continue to grow and reach their full potential.
- Our community that we are part of to reach their full potential.

This has helped us define our purpose and values.

Our purpose is:

FARRAGUT exists to pursue the company's full potential by helping our employees and customers achieve their full potential.

Our values are:

- Courage: Choose honesty and vulnerability even when it is hard
- Synergy: Gather people with diverse talents and ideas to accomplish what cannot be done alone
- Transformation: Learn continuously to realise the full potential of individuals and teams to serve our customers

In our opening conversations, Sucheta and Shail explored this subject with me. Their initial question to me was "What do you think of our declared business purpose?"

I was very conscious of the (then) declaration stated boldly on the company's home page:

FULL POTENTIAL AHEAD: We partner with visionary leaders in search of transformational results.

Powerful and heartfelt though this statement is, I felt it didn't do justice to the amazing work they were doing for the world. "I love the purpose of your business", I challenged, "But I had to read between the lines of your website to find it".

Sucheta and Shail asked me to say more. I explained that I was impressed by the capability of the software they produced to collect more tax revenue from citizens in US communities. I explained how I had made the connection between this functionality and the opportunity for the authorities to provide more funds for better services to the same communities. Alternatively, collecting due revenue from those avoiding payment could also mean the ability to reduce taxes from taxpayers, including many who might struggle to pay.

Fair and efficient systems for the collection of revenue and the provision of services to communities are, for me, essential components of the better world we all seek.

With this knowledge, the senior team at Farragut invited me to engage their people in the conversation. Wordclouds from a workshop held in Summer 2021 are shown in Figures 4.1, 4.2, 4.3 and 4.4. They confirm a journey of purpose, examining it from a range of perspectives, starting with staff and finally with society.

From the perspective of employees, what purpose(s) does your organisation serve?

Identify their purpose and live it

Help build skills   Provide purpose   Create community

Opportunity to grow   Serve clients

Provide employment

Net   Training   Create profit

Help build skills   A's

Grow each day   Learning community

Full potential for all

Figure 4.1 Employees' perspective on purpose.

From the perspective of suppliers, what purpose(s) does your organisation serve?

A source of revenue   Ease of doing business with us

Inspiration   Provide opportunities for growth

Trustworthy and Dependable Customer

Provide software

Learning together   They provide employment   Money

Opportunity   Provide them business

Make the world a better place together

Figure 4.2 Suppliers' perspective on purpose.

90 What is *beyond* sustainability? The six aspirations

From the perspective of clients, what purpose(s) does your organisation serve?

Create easy-to-use software

Grow user base

Make their work easier   Make work easier

Educate

Help citizens   Build   Transition   Servant   Help processes

Serve clients

Create Trust in Taxpayers   Transformation   Simplify

Provide software   Make their work easier

Guidance Implementer   Automation

Accuracy of information

Figure 4.3 Clients' perspective on purpose.

What societal purpose(s) does your organisation serve?

Easy to pay property taxes

Lower tax rates through high collection rates

Modernizing tax processes   Better public services

Serve citizens

Source of Inspiration   Fairness   Using resources effectively

Support county services   Support education

Support community

Create trust in government

Common Good   Fair and equitable taxation

Government contractor

Figure 4.4 Societal purpose.

The above wordclouds capture a quick snapshot of a richer conversation. Notice how moving from an "inward" employee perspective in stages through to profound societal purpose opens the minds of those involved. After the "societal" purpose, we were also able to ask participants which of the UN Sustainable Development Goals (SDGs) were most impacted by the work of Farragut. We discovered that the most impact was made (in order) to the following goals:

1. SDG11: Sustainable cities and communities
2. SDG1: No poverty
3. SDG4: Quality education
4. SDG2: End hunger
5. SDG8: Decent work and economic growth
6. SDG9: Industry, innovation and infrastructure
7. SDG10: Reduced inequalities
8. SDG16: Peace, justice and strong institutions
9. SDG17: Partnership for the goals

People found this realisation inspiring. All of a sudden, their work had shifted from writing software to creating sustainable cities and communities and reducing poverty (etc.). In short, they had become quite clear that their work was contributing significantly to the brighter future we all want. Though they perhaps wouldn't have used these words, the team at Farragut, like so many businesses in our world, is in active pursuit of Abundance.

One thing that seems pretty certain going forward is that we will secure an abundance of clean renewable energy. The only thing that remains uncertain is the time it will take for this to have a significant impact on climate change. The team at RethinkX is confident that economics will drive the price of solar (for example) down so far that it will be compelling and consequently displace the use of fossil fuels at scale. However, there is no time to lose. This is reflected in Adam Dorr's (of RethinkX) inspiring book *Brighter*.

So, we must be thankful for the millions of players in this system who are designing, manufacturing and installing renewable energy systems. Not to mention those working hard simply to reduce energy consumption. Every kW saved is a kW that doesn't need to be generated, and there is

92 What is *beyond* sustainability? The six aspirations

massive scope to save energy and money from doing simple things as my next personal encounter highlights.

PERSONAL ENCOUNTER 4.2 – MIKE KAYE: "ABUNDANT GREEN ENERGY"

Through my work as chair of the United Nations Association (Harrogate Branch),[4] I was approached by a local charity, Zero Carbon Harrogate,[5] focused on accelerating the journey of our hometown to Zero Carbon. I joined their organisation as a member and asked what I could do to help. Knowing my work as a facilitator and coach, they asked if I could support one local business to consciously increase its contribution to Zero Carbon.

Cutting a long story short, I was introduced to Mike Kaye, managing director of Energy Oasis,[6] a local small business focused on energy measurement, energy reduction and renewables. I worked with Mike and his team for over a year to create a new brand and purpose – "intelligent zero-carbon solutions" and a vision for saving vast quantities of CO_2 emissions through their work.

There are several case studies at the Energy Oasis website, but one of my favourites is the installation of intelligent LED lighting in the car park beneath Harrogate Convention Centre.[7] This is one of the largest conference and exhibition centres in the UK. Each year it attracts a variety of people from around the world for trade and exhibition shows as well as for live events and performances.

Energy Oasis was asked by Harrogate Convention Centre, Harrogate Borough Council and the Premier Inn to help reduce energy consumption. The first area highlighted for energy reduction was the main underground car park for the conference centre and the Premier Inn car park. The aim was to reduce running costs, improve the lighting levels to make it safe and accessible to all, make the car park more commercially viable, reduce the associated carbon footprint and eliminate the costly re-lamping exercise every two years.

A UK-manufactured LED lighting solution was chosen to replace the twin fluorescent fittings. Each new fitting was equipped with an integrated passive infrared (PIR) sensor to provide motion detection,

---

maintain light levels and enable daylight harvesting. About 60% of the lights were set to dim down to 10% after two minutes if no motion was detected, and 40% of the fittings were set to turn off after two minutes if no motion was detected.

As a result of the controls in each light, the car park owners saved over 70% on energy consumption compared to the previous lighting solution and an estimated 8.2 tonnes of carbon per year. The choice of fittings was also important to ensure a virtually maintenance-free success rate. Needless to say, the owners were delighted.

What I particularly like about this personal encounter is the scope for vastly more of the same action. There are car parks, owned by local authorities, businesses and other organisations throughout the world with the scope to vastly save energy and reduce climate impact. Mike Kaye sees the scope as enormous:

> Energy reduction is one of the key platforms to reaching Zero Carbon, and the pound you don't have to spend is the easiest one to get back, so change can happen quickly. Using intelligent systems and controls is not new, they cost more initially but the energy and carbon savings not only repay the investment faster, they increase the longevity of the installation. Energy Oasis loves doing projects like this and with current energy prices the return on investment can be less than eight months.

> One thing Mike Kaye and Tesla's Elon Musk have in common is absolute confidence that we can access as much clean renewable energy as the world needs. In fact, according to Tony Seba at the RethinkX think tank in the United States, the trend is for clean energy to be affordable and plentiful within a decade. Of course, that's still not an excuse to waste it. It's not totally clean and cheap – yet!

Hopefully, we've agreed that there is more than enough affordable, renewable energy for the world. But what about food? We frequently hear stories about famine, often in African countries and other places in the so-called "Global South". I am blessed to have encountered one man who is clearly paying no attention to the (bad) news stories. He has discovered that sometimes, it isn't high-tech that we need. Just knowledge, patience and the willingness to work with nature rather than against it.

PERSONAL ENCOUNTER 4.3 – LUWAYO BISWICK: "ABUNDANT FOOD"

A few years ago, thanks to my association with the Open Arms Infants Home in Malawi (it's a long story), I found myself supporting leaders in that country – leaders from banks, not-for-profits and other organisations. On one occasion I was working with local Primeast colleagues to facilitate a "Future Search" three-day workshop for Kusamala, an organisation focused on spreading the opportunities of permaculture – basically working with local ecosystems to grow nutritious food.

During our workshop, we had a hundred farmers and local government and community leaders. We met some amazing people but, for me, one man stood out from the crowd. Luwayo Biswick, who I have come to know affectionately as "Biswick", was part of the Kusamala team. I was impressed by his energy, enthusiasm and leadership qualities.

Biswick left Kusamala to start his own farm which he named "Permaculture Paradise".[8] We have stayed in touch ever since and, on a couple of occasions, I have invited Biswick to tell his story to groups I have been facilitating, including our local branch of the United Nations Association.

A few years ago, on one of our online catchups, Biswick and I got talking about forests. I recall mentioning the role of forests in mitigating climate change. To my surprise, on a later call, Biswick casually mentioned that he had "grown a forest". I was amazed and asked if he and his friends had been planting trees. He simply replied with a comment I shall never forget:

> In Malawi, we don't have to plant trees to make a forest. We simply protect the land from animals and humans and the forest grows.

Since our conversation, Biswick and his team have allowed significant areas of forest to grow. The forests bear fruit and together with other plants that thrive in the natural ecology, they feed local people with abundant nutritious food all year round. Here in one of the world's poorest countries, Biswick affirms that "there is no need for anyone to go hungry".

Today Permaculture Paradise Institute (PPI) is a social enterprise, demonstration and training centre that promotes permaculture systems in Malawi located in Langa village of Mchinji district. Formally established in February 2017, it provides low-cost social economic and ecologically sound training to local farmers, entrepreneurs, nongovernmental organisations as well as government. PPI realises the need for promoting and uplifting the welfare of Malawians and other vulnerable people for the purpose of strengthening family units, alleviating poverty, countering disease and fighting all forms of economic, social, political and religious barriers. It also helps to curb the problem of illiteracy amongst the peasantry population in general through the promotion of informal education. One of PPI's many strengths is the promotion of informal education in Malawi in order to alleviate current predicates and ecological chaos.

Permaculture Paradise was founded by Biswick and his wife Grace Davison. The young couple decided to quit their previous employments to take Permaculture as a full-time business, to create a model and future where majority of the people in Malawi become mind-independent with positive self-esteem that would create possibilities for an effective life.

Their programmes help to address issues to do with hunger, malnutrition, poverty, resource depletion and mitigate issues to do with climate change whilst helping the community generate income by selling produce from the gardens.

Biswick and Grace offer onsite technical support for the implementation of permaculture and agroecology as well as any support customised to client needs. Their products and services are offered and open to all sorts of people according to their background and the context in which they work.

It's not just in the so-called Global South that people go hungry. Here in the UK, there are many families who, for one reason or another, struggle to put food on the table. Approximately 8.4 million people in the UK are in food poverty and, according to BusinessWaste.co.uk, we throw away 9.5 million tonnes of food waste in a single year. When this impacts children, it knocks on to other challenges as well, as Nathan Atkinson (my next personal encounter) discovered.

PERSONAL ENCOUNTER 4.4 – NATHAN ATKINSON: "RETHINK FOOD"

I was first introduced to Nathan Atkinson by Tom Riordan in his role as Chief Executive at Leeds City Council. Tom had been to one of our UNA (Harrogate) meetings in 2016 to share his plans for a more sustainable Leeds. He spoke enthusiastically about the work Nathan was doing to feed children who had been turning up hungry to the school where he had been head teacher. Knowing that he couldn't give an effective education to hungry children, Nathan set about channelling food surplus from wholesale markets, supermarkets and other sources to his school to feed the children.

I invited Nathan to another UNA meeting in 2018, and he shared the headlines of his work with our members. They in turn shared their thoughts and ideas to help make the work even more impactful.

It wasn't long before his initiative was feeding multiple schools in and beyond the Leeds area. The legacy of his initial work transitioned into "Rethink Food"[9] a programme that now engages over 350 schools nationally, supporting children and their families to live food-secure lives.

Rethink Food is now a mature curriculum enrichment programme that provides educational support and resources to assist schools in teaching food-based learning all linked to the United Nations SDGs. The project is passionate about educating children, business and communities to love food and care for the environment. It has three objectives:

1. Remove hunger as a barrier to learning
2. Reduce the amount of perfectly edible food that goes to waste
3. Educate communities to make responsible choices about food for a sustainable future

I caught up with Nathan again in 2023 to see how he was getting on. His programme goes from strength to strength. You can view my conversation with Nathan on the "Leading Beyond Sustainability" playlist on my YouTube channel.

A spirit of abundance **97**

I have come to admire people who see an issue and directly innovate to resolve it. However, the transformation of our world is very much a team effort, within and between organisations. My next encounter features a human resources and coaching professional who was intent on bringing her services into play in support of organisations that make the world a better place.

PERSONAL ENCOUNTER 4.5 – DEBBIE CONNORS: "NURTURING ABUNDANCE THROUGH POSITIVITY IN PEOPLE SYSTEMS"

The tough decision for this personal encounter was knowing which chapter to put it in. I have known Debbie[10] for the best part of 20 years. We met through local branch meetings of the Chartered Institute of Personnel and Development. At around that time, Debbie was HR Manager at McCain Foods in the UK. She and I had both given talks at branch meetings. So, I could easily have placed this in Chapter 1 to emphasise Debbie's natural tendency to connect.

Over the years, Debbie and I have met regularly to catch up, compare notes and do a bit of co-coaching with each other. Chapter 2 (Peace) could equally have been a good home for Debbie's story as her focus is often on how to deal compassionately with conflict in the workplace. In fact, she has described her coaching and human resources work as "utilising generative coaching to deliver a different kind of HR". As we will explore further in Part II of this book, generative coaching and generative listening are core skills for working with other people with "an ear to the emerging future". Debbie combines the use of "clean language" in her methods to ensure she isn't leading her colleagues and clients down a path that is not entirely their own.

Debbie also weaves well-being into her personal life and service, always keen to help people find the right balance for themselves to do justice to all parts of their lives. Clearly a Chapter 3 trait promoting vitality for herself and others.

So, here we are in Chapter 4 focusing on abundance. Debbie has a powerful "abundance mindset". She has a personal passion for sustainability and for supporting others on that path. She was a great encourager for me when she realised I was writing this book.

98 What is *beyond* sustainability? The six aspirations

Despite being a natural "freelancer", Debbie's passion for a brighter future has prompted her to take a senior HR role in a company specialising in solar energy and which has experienced hyper growth in recent times as the world exploits this technology as a key contributory solution to the climate crisis.

Not being content to "do the basics" as an HR leader, Debbie is keen to make sure her employer plays its maximum role in the provision of clean, cost-effective and abundant energy. She knows instinctively that this will not happen without wise leadership and a profound strategic understanding of how the global energy infrastructure will evolve at lightening pace over the coming decade or so. This requires transformational leadership that Debbie is determined to influence through her role as an HR leader and trusted partner to the executive. In a world where simply responding to inevitable demand will certainly ensure massive short-term gains, Debbie is keen to focus the minds of leaders on the bigger picture. Questions such as the following have been inspiring topics of conversation during our recent meetings:

1. Even with all the materials and equipment available for energy transformation, how do we ensure that skills from installation to consultancy keep pace with demand?
2. How do we ensure that the solar industry meets the other demands of a world that is becoming increasingly aware of supply chain ethics?
3. How does the solar industry integrate with the wider energy distribution system so that providing generation close to demand can alleviate the need for expensive grid reinforcement?
4. How does the solar industry positively support the integration of multiple technologies that will inevitably be a feature of the modern world very soon: electric vehicles, battery storage, green hydrogen, other storage systems (gravity, heat, hydro to name just three more)?
5. What to do with over-generation that might become an important issue and opportunity as solar grows to meet demand even in winter months?

Let's face it; these are not typical questions being posed by an HR professional (no disrespect intended). But they are critical to the leadership development and people strategies that will be imperative for the most successful players in this sector.

So, you can see how easy it would have been also to have featured Debbie and her work in Chapter 5 on Opportunity and Chapter 6 on Wisdom.

I admire greatly Debbie's ability to continue her independent work as a consultant and generative coach alongside her corporate HR role. Her inspiration and energy are definitely a force for good in the world.

It seems the conversations I had with Debbie resonated, so much so that, just as this book was nearing completion, Debbie sent me the following words to add to her personal encounter. However, I was so inspired by them that I decided to include them as an activity for you, the reader. Take the time to read Debbie's words (that follow below) in a quiet, uninterrupted space. Pause for contemplation after each paragraph and follow Debbie's general guidance. There are inevitably many links to the other five aspirations – you may wish to note them and add your other thoughts to your journal.

ACTIVITY FROM DEBBIE CONNORS: "CONTEMPLATING ABUNDANCE"

We live in a world of abundance. Abundance is within and without. Yet when we consider abundance in our own lives, our minds may automatically think of the accumulation of material wealth and resources over other areas of bounty. Individuals may prioritise different aspects based on their values, beliefs and life circumstances all of which is a version of reality but not necessarily the truth.

There are many ways of thinking about abundance depending on your perception and state of mind.

A person with a high level of antibodies in their body that keeps them healthy against viruses may be time-poor and not recognise their abundance of health. Our own bodies are abundant, made up of trillions of atoms and more neural networks than there are grains of sand on the planet, we have billions of blood cells and DNA that holds trillions of bits of information. Even if we had nothing else outside of our bodies, depending on your perspective, we are abundant.

Our planet, Gaia, is abundant – it gives freely its oxygen, carbon dioxide, food, animals, oceans rivers, water, nature, beauty from which we all benefit and without which we could not exist.

We have economies, shops, technology, roads, railways, trains, cars, inventors, music, art, clothes, movies, medicines, hospitals – more resources on the planet than ever.

As you read this book, whether you are sitting in a café, a park or a comfortable or very modest place that you call your home – there is abundance and beauty all around us – just stop and look – what do you see?

In the end, it's about perception, a state of mind and the feelings it generates. At the end of the day, abundance is just a word that we give meaning to. If you think of yourself as lacking, then that's what you will experience. If you see yourself as abundant, then that's what you will experience. As the saying goes: "what you focus on grows".

Our world is teeming with abundance, and it starts with you. Consider your life to date, your experiences, the make-up of your body. Don't judge anything, just notice with wonder and amazement how far you've come, the world in which you exist. Be present in the feeling of abundance because there is only the present moment which is the power of now.

Finally, it's a practice and even a reprogramming of how you think and perceive. It's up to you, it's always been up to you, and it always will be your choice.

And so, we come to my last encounter in this chapter. I'd like to return to the significant aspiration of abundant energy.

PERSONAL ENCOUNTER 4.6 – TONY TOWNLEY: "SMART METERING"

Once upon a time in the 1990s, I was responsible for the "metering assets" at Yorkshire Electricity. My job involved the choice, purchase, distribution, repair and testing of electricity meters, including dealing with (reducing) instances of meter tampering by unscrupulous consumers.

When I first met Tony Townley,[11] he was sales manager for Siemens. He has since worked for many major players in the world of electricity metering and has taken an interest in recent years in the power of SMART metering. He and I have had several inspiring conversations about the potentially critical role SMART metering can play in the move towards a future of renewables and electric transport.

SMART metering isn't new. In the 1990s, we were already exploring its potential and running trials. When most users in the UK think of SMART meters, they think about the associated counter-top displays that inform people how much electricity (and gas) they are using. The logic being that this educates people to consume less and, if they have multiple tariffs, to use electricity when it is cheaper to do so. This is definitely a good thing but only really scrapes the top of yet another very big iceberg.

When combined with home automation (the SMART home), data from a SMART meter can determine the best time to switch circuits on and off for all sorts of reasons.

One of the most common arguments against the electrification of vehicles and renewable energy is that our national grid and distribution system can't cope with the inevitably higher demand for electricity. Also, if power is sourced from wind generation located around the UK coast, new, heavy-duty lines are required to carry the associated current to the places it gets consumed, including the rising demand for car charging.

In a worst-case scenario, all this is true. But think again. We live in an age where it's feasible for a domestic dwelling to use solar and batteries, including our car batteries (still on board the vehicle) to meet 100% of that dwelling's energy needs. It's easy to see how in this example, the need to enhance the grid and distribution system could be completely removed.

But these are two ends of a big spectrum. At the one end, we have remote generation and high consumption at the point of use. At the other, we have generation and consumption perfectly matched at the point of use – and no distribution necessary.

The latter case may be somewhat utopian. Nevertheless, it isn't hard to imagine a scenario where SMART metering is an integral part of an intelligent system that prices energy and switches circuits on and off to the benefit of the consumer and in such a way as to minimise any distribution system or grid overload. In this world, local (probably solar and small-scale wind) generation is encouraged by price incentives, as is storage and even supply back to the system when there is high local demand and perhaps the sun isn't shining.

I am always inspired by Tony's thinking on SMART metering. In November 2023, I caught up with him again just as he was about to transition his career from SMART metering for energy systems to SMART metering for water services. As always, he was as optimistic for the associated environmental benefits in this sector as he has been for energy. We even discussed the possibility of utilising the technology for metering sewage systems. All this was recorded and is available on my YouTube channel.

Chapter summary

Who are the individuals you know of who are making the resources we need, including food, water, energy, services and wealth available – "sufficient for everyone's need and no-one's greed"?

Make a note of your top six (notice), preferably those where you have some kind of personal connection. Check them out online and post a suitable case study of your own on social media (celebrate) with your own words of encouragement. If you're struggling (which I doubt very much), then check out some of the cases in this chapter and simply post their work online.

And what about you? Make a note of six things you're already doing to deliver this aspiration of abundance. Then make a note of six more things you'd like to do in the future – preferably in your diary on the date you're going to make a start.

Guest poem

On 13 September 2023, I caught up with Dr Matt Walsh – remember him from one of my personal encounters in our Chapter 3 on Vitality? He

A spirit of abundance **103**

dropped me a line with a beautiful poem on Abundance – which he wrote on a trip he had just had to France to meet with friends and where the guests had given the host a pear tree. It seems the perfect way to round off this chapter. Enjoy.

Dear Clive,

Here's the poem that I read to you – it is entitled "Pear Tree", and it is about abundance – the pear tree being an ancient symbol of abundance, sustenance and longevity. Matt.

Pear Tree

May your roots grow deep
And find deep springs of sustenance
To keep you healthy and strong

May your leaves be broad and plentiful
Providing generous shade and safe shelter
To all who visit here.

May your timber be fine and your branches tall,
So that you become a landmark for all
who are seeking kindness.
May the winters be gentle with you.

May sweet scented blossom
Glow bright on this tree each spring
To remind the world
about the beauty of friendship.

And in the autumn,
may your abundant seeds scatter far and wide
To make this world a better place

And in the years ahead

May this tree come to represent
Companionship, love, healing
and the wonder of the kindred spirit.[12]

Notes

1 Wilson, C. A. 2024. Poem "Abundance" by Author.
2 Wikipedia, 2024. *Small Is Beautiful*: https://en.wikipedia.org/wiki/Small_Is_Beautiful
3 Farragut Systems Inc, 2022. Farragut: www.farragut.com/
4 United Nations Association, 2024. UNA (Harrogate): https://una.org.uk/branch/una-harrogate
5 Zero Carbon Harrogate, 2024. Zero Carbon Harrogate: www.zerocarbonharrogate.org.uk/
6 Energy Oasis Ltd, 2024. Energy Oasis: www.energyoasis.org.uk/
7 Harrogate Convention Centre, 2024. Harrogate Convention Centre: www.harrogateconventioncentre.co.uk/
8 Permaculture Paradise Insitute, 2024. Permaculture Paradise Institute: https://neverendingfood.org/permaculture-paradise-institute/
9 Rethink Food Limited, 2023. Rethink Food: www.rethinkfood.co.uk/
10 Linked In, 2024. Debbie Connors: www.linkedin.com/in/debbieaconnors/
11 Linked In, 2024. Tony Townley: www.linkedin.com/in/anthony-townley-/
12 Walsh, Dr. M. 2024. Poem "Pear Tree" by kind permission Matt Walsh.

Infinite opportunity 5

Opportunity

> Once upon a time
> A darker time
> We struggled and toiled
> And suffered and wept
>
> But today things are different
> Things are magnificent
> Learning is abundant
> Skills are there for the taking
> A brighter world is in the making
>
> We have the ability
> To avoid fragility
> By bringing our best self into play
> And then to rest in tranquility[1]

Increasing the opportunity for learning and contribution for everyone is key to delivering and enjoying our brighter future. A critical thread will be how we consciously align education and career opportunity to our vision of six aspirations.

DOI: 10.4324/9781003428121-7

106 What is *beyond* sustainability? The six aspirations

ACTIVITY

What clues can we find to the growth of opportunity at "Our World in Data"? Check out the trends in education, literacy and the availability of knowledge to the world's population, often at the click of a mouse. This is clearly an aspiration that is hurtling forward at the speed of light. But it's also quite a scary aspiration for many. Think of those whose jobs get replaced by automation, robotics and artificial intelligence (AI). What thoughts do you have about how we make sure (to quote the United Nations) "no one is left behind"?

As we have said throughout this book, the coming decade will see unprecedented disruption. Many jobs that are commonplace now are likely to be displaced by automation and AI, supported by cheaper renewable energy. Farming also is likely to be significantly disrupted as meat and other animal products move away from the slaughterhouse in favour of much cheaper replacements from new technologies such as precision fermentation and cellular agriculture. This is just the tip of the iceberg. To put it bluntly, many taxi drivers, call-centre staff, farmers and others will probably be looking for and choosing either retirement or exciting alternative careers.

It will be increasingly important for people to notice some of the obvious disruption heading our way and plan for change. Of course, planning for change is nothing new. In fact, some businesses can tell inspiring stories of helping their people to prepare for uncertainty.

PERSONAL ENCOUNTER 5.1 – JEN USHER: "PERSONAL DEVELOPMENT FOR EMPLOYEES' CAREERS BEYOND THEIR TIME WITH THE COMPANY"

Jen Usher is Head of Learning and Development (Global) at Computershare.[2] I first met Jen in 2006 when she was Learning and Development Manager with HML (Home Loan Management Limited), then a subsidiary of Skipton Building Society. My Primeast colleagues and I have worked with and alongside Jen as consultants in leadership on various initiatives since then. But the most inspiring encounter (for me) was seeing how Jen tackled the tricky issue of staff retention during her time as Talent Manager (2011–2013) with UK Asset Resolution Limited,[3] known more widely as UKAR.

UKAR was a government-owned holding company formed following the collapse of Bradford and Bingley and Northern Rock building societies. In effect, this holding company had the sole purpose of collecting the outstanding help-to-buy mortgage debt on behalf of HM Treasury. The business was precluded from other business ventures which meant that the employees of UKAR would be released from employment progressively over the term of the outstanding debts.

So, in a nutshell, the challenge facing Jen as Talent Manager was "how to retain and motivate staff to perform, despite knowing their careers would inevitably end within a foreseeable timeline". To help in this quest, I had the privilege of facilitating a "Talent Forum" for Jen where we invited people professionals from other businesses to support her using "Action Learning Sets" (a renowned group problem-solving methodology first introduced in the 1940s by Reg Revans, a Welshman, university professor and management consultant who had seen his father adopt a similar method during his investigation of the sinking of the Titanic).

Jen already had ideas of how to resolve the issue but wanted to test them with her supporters at the Forum. It was a delight to witness the generous support freely given by fellow professionals whose only gain was to be part of the associated learning. In that respect, I could have easily written this "personal encounter" in the first chapter as a powerful playing out of "Connection", but the real impact was the way Jen ultimately supported the provision of career "Opportunity" for staff at UKAR.

Consequent to Jen's courageous problem solving and the generosity of other professionals to be involved, Jen instigated a "Progressive Talent Management Strategy" where staff were actively supported to think about their careers through UKAR and beyond and to be sponsored for personal development that would effectively bring their "best-selves" into service of the world of work generally.

My next "personal encounter" builds on the theme of personal development. About 20 years ago, I was quite outspoken on the subject of talent and talent management. I can remember being a keynote speaker at numerous

108 What is *beyond* sustainability? The six aspirations

conferences and proclaiming that "Talent doesn't need to be managed – it needs to be liberated!".

This bold attitude went against the prevailing thinking at the time – that talent was scarce and needed to be captured, developed and retained. This so-called "War for Talent" led to the concept of "Hi-po's", that top 10% or so of the workforce with "high potential" who needed to be treated as special cases. I spoke passionately that everyone has talent and that leaders have a responsibility to liberate and develop each person's talent by investing in proportion to perceived potential. I wrote a small text on "Talent Liberation" and taught for ten years a programme for HR leaders at the Chartered Institute of Personnel and Development[4] which went under the banner of "Progressive Strategies for Talent Management". During this time, I engaged with hundreds of HR directors and heads of Talent Management and Learning and Development. One of my star participants is at the centre of my next "encounter".

PERSONAL ENCOUNTER 5.2 – CATHY: "PUTTING PEOPLE IN THE DRIVER'S SEAT OF THEIR CAREERS"

The year 2020, as everyone knows, was the year we were first hit with the global impact of the Covid-19 pandemic. It began a period of significant acceleration in the field of digital payments, enabling the world's population to buy more goods and services online and also to avoid cash transactions (and thereby avoid transmission of the virus) even with local shops and service providers.

To keep pace with these demands, one major global business in the world of digital payments wanted to improve performance through the empowerment of their people.

I had the good fortune to be working closely with Cathy, the company's director of Learning and Development. She and her colleagues had designed a method to provide everyone in the company the opportunity to truly own their own development, performance and well-being. The rationale for this move was centred around the belief and evidence that, if people could consciously stay well and play to their personal strengths in pursuit of career aims they truly believed in, they would bring the best of who they were to work, improve performance and enjoy personal success in the process.

The challenge facing Cathy and her colleagues was to shift a global corporate culture from one where managers often led the way to one where individual team members could take "the driver's seat of their own career". The company made meaningful investments in the systems and processes to support the change but, as is often the case, additional work was needed for the associated shift in attitudes, beliefs, skills and behaviours.

Team members at all levels had to learn what empowerment truly felt like and understand how to think through and implement personal changes in their own best interests and that of the company. Leaders and managers similarly had to adjust their approach, cultivate supportive relationships and encourage their people to take ownership.

At that time, the company employed some 24,000 team members, including 4,000 managers. So, to complete the challenge in just one year required considerable determination, ingenuity and technology.

In many ways, the pandemic was accelerating the ability for large numbers of people to engage rapidly online. Consequently, videoconferencing and polling software were adopted to allow people to share their thoughts and experiences at webinars of up to a thousand people at once, and we also devised virtual instructor-led training (VILT) for managers to explore how best to support the change.

To support these interactive events and make additional learning available to team members in a flexible manner, my colleagues in the Learning and Design Studio at Primeast also created and delivered a comprehensive curriculum of eLearning modules. This meant people could further learn and practice new skills fit for their future career journeys.

Since this one-year programme, the company has been monitoring the difference it has made.

Cathy was impressed by the rate of adoption of this new approach. In the first year of the programme, 64% of team members had participated; the forecast for 2023 is 82% and the target for 2024 is 95%. However, more important than the numbers involved, Cathy had this to say about the impact on the company and especially on its people:

This new approach is developing a culture of conversation and individual ownership of performance and results. It is opening up more future-focused conversations, encouraging employees to talk about what they need to be successful. Our formal measurement of the eLearning showed that over 90% of our people found it to be engaging and relevant to their role. Consequently, they reported that they were significantly more confident in getting the most from conversations on well-being, development and performance. I am certain that the initial online events allowing two-way engagement accelerated the adoption and impact of the new approach and in turn increased the focus on personal development opportunity for the vast majority of our people.

I'm writing this chapter at a time when there is so much speculation in the press about the forthcoming impact of AI. There is absolutely no doubt that AI will transform society in so many ways, including driverless vehicles, SMART homes, the production of content (articles, books, video, music, etc.), more sophisticated and personalised health care, retail, banking and learning. The list is endless. I am excited about the gains to humanity and sincerely hope the downside of fake news; social media misinformation and numerous other ills will be regulated and controlled.

My next "personal encounter" is just a taste of the benefits of AI in education and learning generally.

PERSONAL ENCOUNTER 5.3 – FERGUS HAMILTON: "MAKING AI WORK FOR SCHOOLS"

As affirmed by Steven Pinker and others, we live in a world where vastly more young people receive education than ever before. Consequently, according to the World Economic Forum, 87% of the global population over the age of 14 is now able to read and write, compared to 17% two centuries ago. The greatest increases have been recorded since World War II.

Despite these increases, humanity has an insatiable quest to further improve the education of young people and provide greater opportunity for them to lead their greatest lives. Close to home, I recently enjoyed a holiday in Northumberland with a small group of family and friends, including Fergus Hamilton.

Since graduating from the University of Cambridge in 2013, Fergus has led an impressive career of service to humanity, including work with UK International Aid to galvanise action to tackle female genital mutilation and child early and forced marriage. He also led a nutrition capacity-building project with Government of Tanzania in Dodoma and Tanga on behalf of the UN World Food Programme and consulted on finance, healthcare and social impact with the Boston Consulting Group.

Fergus is now head of Strategy and Customer Success for Century Tech,[5] a high-growth, AI-driven ed-tech platform. His work is to lead and develop his team to support schools and colleges around the world in order to get the most from cutting-edge technology.

I was fascinated to hear how, for example, AI is being used to enable a teaching and learning platform for primary and secondary schools, colleges and universities. The company uses learning science, AI and neuroscience to create constantly adapting pathways for students and powerful assessment data for teachers.

These solutions facilitate learning and growth opportunities for learners in such an intimate and customised way that would be difficult and time-consuming for already busy teachers.

Given that AI is very much in its infancy and despite obvious concerns over its potential misuse, I am excited at the massive opportunities it presents. I guess, like many of us, I have often thought of improvements in education being associated with reaching more young people than in previous years, but Fergus's work has caused me to reflect that the impact of education is as much (if not more) about quality and personal choice as it is simply about scale and numbers of people reached.

In a way, my next personal encounter links right back to the first chapter when I talked about the power of Connection. One of the young leaders I met at the United Nations Youth Action Summit in New York was Federico Restrepo, usually known as Fede. He was one of a team of young leaders who initiated the project "Youth for Global Goals" to bring the UN SDGs to every young person on the planet.

112 What is *beyond* sustainability? The six aspirations

PERSONAL ENCOUNTER 5.4 – FEDERICO RESTREPO: "OPPORTUNITIES FOR SUSTAINABLE START-UPS"

I wrote about Fede's amazing work to promote the SDGs in my book, *Designing the Purposeful World*. But I felt sure, knowing Fede's infectious enthusiasm, that that was just the start of an exciting journey.

I caught up with Fede[6] in 2022 and was keen to know what he had been up to since our last conversation in 2017. Well, I wasn't disappointed.

When Fede discovered that his young niece Milagros had a lung disease, he set out to discover what caused it. He examined evidence from a study at Kings College in London which suggested that air pollution was the probable cause, not just for Milagros, but for many other people where he lived in Columbia.

He also discovered that the pollution was, in turn, mainly caused by internal combustion engines used in cars and other vehicles. So, he decided to begin a new start-up to electrify vehicles. When I spoke with him, his team had successfully converted over 50 vehicles.

But that wasn't all, Fede had hoped to gain the support of a business incubator to set up his business. He discovered that support was really only available for start-ups in computing and associated technologies. So, he did what Fede would do. He started his own incubator, "Impact Hub Medellin" which readers can find out more about at the website. At the time of our conversation, the Hub was employing a team of 22 people and had supported over a thousand new businesses, all aligned with the UN SDGs. In the years to come, Fede has the ambition to bring such opportunities to many more start-ups in Columbia and beyond.

When I contemplate my journey through secondary education and into the world of work as a teenager in inner-city Leeds, I am conscious that my early career choices were down to a few chance encounters with family and neighbours. Compare that hap-hazard strategy for career commencement to the far more thoughtful and well-planned approach alluded to in my next encounter.

PERSONAL ENCOUNTER 5.5 – FRANCESCA WALKER-MARTIN: "PRACADEMICS"

I first met Fran in 2014 when she was Senior Lecturer (Employability Lead) and LaunchPad Lead at the University of Central Lancashire (UCLan),[7] as well as Approved Centre Director for the Chartered Management Institute (CMI).[8] Fran invited me to speak at one of her LaunchPad events at UCLan, aimed at inspiring students to build on their further education and embark on purposeful careers that would add meaning for themselves and value to the world. She knew me as a Fellow of CMI and because of my (then) upcoming book *Designing the Purposeful Organization*.

Fran is a Reader in work-based learning in the *School of Business* at UCLan, teaching a range of students from undergraduate to post-graduate. She has a specific commitment to providing them with the best possible work-based learning experience, including research-informed teaching.

In 2017, she enhanced her portfolio by adding Degree Apprenticeships and is now Degree Apprentice Lead with a focus on quality in line with Ofsted, QAA and OfS requirements. As a Chartered Member of the CMI and Senior Fellow of the Higher Education Academy, Fran has grown a wide network of colleagues who provide support and guidance to her students. I'm honoured to be part of this network.

Since my first engagement at UCLan, I have returned several times to engage with students and businesses at UCLan, as well as at the ASET[9] national conference. I have always admired Fran's passion for work-based learning, something that plays out enthusiastically in her role as chair of ASET. It has clearly been a key driver in her working life. She knows first-hand that students who engage with the offer of this experience will transform, often beyond their wildest dreams. In turn, they make the world a far better place.

I love the way Fran refers to those who integrate education and workplace experience as "Pracademics". It's one of those custom words which, once learned, is unforgettable.

I was curious to hear some of Fran's most inspiring stories of young people finding their purpose and making the world a better place. So, I caught up with her in October 2023 and she shared the following:

114   What is *beyond* sustainability? The six aspirations

The thing about this job is that you're on a long burn. The "stuff" that we teach is not always for now as the students or learners have not yet experienced the relevant situation to apply that piece of learning. But, the joy of my job is the passing of time. I have lost count of the number of times that I have received emails texts and messages (often years after students have graduated), that say, "I get it now!" and "thank you – I am now using …!".

My work is all about building the leaders of the future – I play a tiny part in that journey, but I argue that getting the foundations right pays it forward. There are leaders out there now doing amazing jobs and leading amazing teams who are all making the world a better place. How good is that!

Sometimes in life, you are privileged to be there at a magical moment. I was there at the very moment that one of my students, who had come to education via a nontraditional route, discovered what they wanted to do in the world. They wanted to become a lecturer. I saw this magic happen as my student presented their final-year research findings at a national conference. When they left the auditorium they said, "I want to teach".

It has been nine years since that moment and those have been years of graft, balancing work and a family of four whilst gaining new qualifications, undertaking major research, writing book chapters and delivering hundreds of lectures to anxious or knowledge-hungry students. My student is now an internationally recognised Senior Lecturer who supports, guides and inspires students, pracademics and their own children.

I love my job!

Chapter summary

Who are the individuals or organisations you know of who are actively providing or facilitating opportunity for others to learn and make their best contribution?

Make a note of your top six (notice), preferably those where you have some kind of personal connection. Check them out online and post a suitable case study of your own on social media (celebrate) with your own words of encouragement. If you're struggling (which I doubt very much) then check out some of the cases in this chapter and simply post their work online.

And what about you? Make a note of six things you're already doing to facilitate learning and opportunity for contribution. Then make a note of six more things you'd like to do in the future – preferably in your diary on the date you're going to start.

Notes

1 Wilson, C. A. 2024. Poem "Opportunity" by Author.
2 Computershare Limited, 2024. Computershare: www.computershare.com/uk
3 UK Asset Resolution Limited, 2024. UKAR: www.ukar.co.uk/
4 The Chartered Institute of Personnel and Development, 2024. CIPD: www.cipd.org/uk
5 Century-Tech Limited, 2024. Century: www.century.tech/about-us/
6 Linked In, 2024. Federico Restrepo Sierra: www.linkedin.com/in/federicorestrepos/
7 The University of Central Lancashire, 2024. UCLAN: www.uclan.ac.uk/
8 Chartered Management Institute, 2024. CMI: www.managers.org.uk/
9 ASET, The Work Based Learning and Placement Learning Association, 2023. ASET: www.asetonline.org/

Profound wisdom 6

Wisdom

The secret of wisdom
Is living for today
And for tomorrow
With one eye on the moment
And another on eternity

To plant the tree today
Knowing without sorrow
Someone else may lay
In its shade tomorrow

To give without measure
Or ration
Or expectation
Any treasure
Simply knowing
Someone's day will be brighter

To know the difference
Between creation and reaction
To pause before speaking
To make sure of traction

DOI: 10.4324/9781003428121-8

To live simply
But fully
In love with the whole world[1]

Our sixth and final aspiration is wisdom. This is a critical and profound aspiration and so necessary to delivering our brighter future. It is the only aspiration from the six which doesn't comprise the aims and objectives of the UN Sustainable Development Goals (SDGs), although it could be argued that it is a thread that weaves through all 17 SDGs. This key chapter also provides a hook to Part III of this book, "The Wisdom Code", which will discuss the topic of Wisdom in much more depth, exploring why it is so important at this particular moment in the history of humanity, what wise leadership might look like and how to systematically develop wisdom amongst leaders of today and of tomorrow.

As a reminder, my choice of the six aspirations for this book came about as a result of two experiences.

The first experience was my engagement with thousands of people aged from seven to well over 70 across the four continents of Europe, North America, Africa and Asia. My invitation to audiences at my workshops was simple – to close our eyes and envisage the world we would like to see in 2030. Granted this was in order to engage them on the subject of the UN SDGs – but this intention was not declared at the outset of any workshop.

The second was a practice I have come to value more and more as I get older, that of contemplation. I was encouraged in my practice of contemplation by watching the YouTube video "Contemplation – The Most Important Tool For Sages" by Leo Gura.[2] Leo explains at length the need to take time away from other people's content to establish a personal perspective on things that matter to us. This is not to say that we shouldn't learn from others, it's simply to say that we *also* need to search deep inside our own consciousness to establish profound meaning.

I have met many wise leaders and teachers in my lifetime of 68 years and counting. I have had the privilege of working with many of them, and several have already been mentioned in earlier chapters and the personal case studies therein. So, coming up with a new six without duplication proved to be difficult.

Also, as this book is about *Leading Beyond Sustainability*, I was curious to explore the concept of wise organisations. Is there such a thing? So, in the age of Artificial Intelligence, I thought I'd consult chat.openai.com and see

118 What is *beyond* sustainability? The six aspirations

what GPT had to say on the topic. This is what I was told when I asked, "Can an organisation be wise?"

> An organisation, in and of itself, doesn't possess wisdom like an individual does. However, the collective actions, decisions and culture of an organisation can reflect wisdom when they demonstrate sound judgement, ethical behaviour and the ability to learn from experience. Wisdom is often attributed to the people within an organisation who make thoughtful choices and lead with integrity. So, while organisations don't inherently possess wisdom, they can certainly exhibit it through the actions and values of their members.

I have contemplated this statement, and it leaves me undecided. In my previous books on purpose, I have spoken about fractals, suggesting that an organisation is a life form a level of scale higher than the individual and a level of scale below that of humanity which is also a life form. And, just as individuals have a "character" formed of their beliefs, values and behaviours, so does an organisation have a "character" or "culture" formed from the values brought to it by the individuals associated with it. Interestingly, in my experience, the cultures diagnosed in most organisations I have worked with have not been as constructive as the combined values of those who work there. Cultures form over time and can become toxic despite the good intentions of the contributors. We know only too well that it takes time and determination to create a culture in an organisation that is as good as, or even better than, the sum of its parts.

A chain is as strong as its weakest link

This truth is worth contemplating. Think about it, the way we usually regard a chain is as a set of links in series, held in tension by the work in hand. However, if we were to place multiple similar chains in parallel, we could strengthen their performance greater than that of any one chain.

Aren't culture and wisdom a bit like this?

Isn't it the case that an organisation functioning well and displaying great teamwork could have an even more constructive culture than the sum of its parts? Similarly, wisdom isn't a "one size fits all" concept. People can be very wise at dealing with finances and still be clumsy (or unwise) in the way they deal with relationships or conflict. Surely a truly wise organisation will play to (and learn from) its "wisdom" strengths as much as it will to any other strength.

Why does this matter?

This matters a great deal. The whole of Part II of this book asks us to contemplate which character we play in the quest for a brighter future. Which link in the chain are we? It also encourages us to seek out and collaborate wisely with characters who differ from ourselves. Working in silos, whether in our organisations or in the world, will not take us to our brighter future as efficiently as by working together.

ACTIVITY

What data can you find on the evolution of wisdom at "Our World in Data"? Take a look and make your own journal notes.

Clearly, there could well be links to the growth in education and knowledge as discussed in the previous chapter. And we can find data to confirm that, on average, people are living longer. Coupled to that, we know that wisdom is often born through years of experience.

For trends, encouraging and otherwise, we may have to look a little further.

One source for exploration is the work of Richard Barrett, founder of the Barrett Values Centre and the Barrett Academy for the Advancement of Human Values. Richard is also the author of many books, including one book that I found most helpful in my own learning: *Worldview Dynamics and the Well-Being of Nations*.[3]

And so, I come to my personal encounters with wisdom from my life's journey. As in the earlier chapters, these are all people who have struck me as being wise and who have been catalysts to my own development. I am in eternal gratitude to them and to the quirks of life that have allowed me to find them.

PERSONAL ENCOUNTER 6.1 – PHIL CLOTHIER: "WISDOM BORN OF LOVE"

I met Phil Clothier and Tor Eneroth through my work at Primeast and our use of Richard Barrett's "seven levels of human consciousness model" which can easily be found and explored online.[4]

When I first met Phil, he was CEO of Barrett Values Centre. This was more than a decade ago. Over the years, Phil has shared key moments of his life with me. I have learnt how he grew up surrounded by hundreds of foster "brothers and sisters" in the children's homes run by his parents. These children had often experienced trauma and abandonment before joining their new "family". Phil and the other children were actively and purposefully involved in making newcomers feel at home and able to deal with their human needs.

In his adult life, Phil encountered the Barrett model and method, first from reading one of Richard's early textbooks and then from taking a Personal Values Assessment and discussing his report directly with Richard. A personal insight from that experience was realising that one of the values he had chosen (being liked) was potentially limiting if it proved to be more important than living with integrity.

Phil later took the reins of Barrett Values Centre as its chief executive, and I had the good fortune to work with him on several occasions and in various guises. Amongst all this we have climbed a few hills together and, during the global pandemic, regularly collaborated on various projects, including one to measure the cultural shift in workplaces, directly prompted by lockdown. As we both suspected, the shift had been significant. We saw a shift in chosen values that would normally take about five years – in just as many weeks!

Over the years I have known Phil, he has had to deal with a number of personal challenges, all of which I witnessed him doing in a spirit of openness, collaboration with others and wisdom. Always accepting of the "now" at a personal and societal level, Phil nevertheless plays a significant part in what I would call the "transformation of human consciousness".

Phil was the first person I ever knew outside my family to weave the word "love" into every conversation. He describes "love" as his highest value, and this shines through absolutely everything he does, from litter picking, being with his family, working in his local community and sharing deep wisdom on the world stage.

This next personal encounter is deliberately sequenced after that of Phil Clothier above, simply because of the order in which I met him and Tor. I could easily have rolled these two accounts into one but, in the end decided to make them two – somewhat joined at the hip.

PERSONAL ENCOUNTER 6.2 – TOR ENEROTH: "WISDOM THROUGH ATTENTIVE LISTENING"

Tor grew up in Sweden and was deeply loved by his family. However, he once showed me an early childhood photograph where he was in what appeared to be a cage. He explained that he was there due to his hyperactivity. The cage was part of his bed and was locked to prevent Tor from waking the rest of the family at hourly intervals during the night.

Like Phil, Tor made the connection to his childhood experiences by exploring his Barrett values profile. He began to understand how his personal energy and enthusiasm were linked to a personal sense of not being good enough and the desire to constantly prove himself. This continued into his adult life where he had been working eighty-hour weeks in order to feel able to contribute to society.

I've worked closely with Tor a number of times, sometimes with Phil and sometimes just the two of us. On one occasion, we were both coaching senior partners at a well-known global consultancy. The part of the firm we were working with had completed a Company Values Assessment and we were working with their top professionals to help them collectively make the shift to wiser ways of working and being.

I remember receiving much wisdom from Tor on that particular assignment. I had been a Barrett practitioner for many years, but sharing our different approaches in service of our client was invaluable. I remember being inspired by the way Tor described his approach to debriefing an individual assessment. He would set the tone by sharing enough of his own life story to allow his clients to be at ease and encouraged to share what had made them "the leader you are today".

> Tor's patient and calm approach made my work so much easier. By the time I got around to showing my clients their report, I already knew much of who they truly were and also why they were that way.
>
> Tor was involved alongside Phil in much of our recent collaboration, including the assessment of workplace cultural shift associated with the pandemic.
>
> I had thought about conducting an interview with Tor and Phil separately to supplement these two personal case studies with more insights from them on the subject of wisdom. Instead, I chose to seek an interview with them both together. If you'd like to get to know these wise men a little better, you can be a "fly on the wall" to our conversation on my YouTube channel.

A short while ago, when Phil and Tor from the above "encounters" were setting up their wonderful new venture, Amcara, I chose to write a short poem for each of them. I hope you enjoy them and, through this medium, get to feel their wisdom.

"And" (for Phil)

And
As the wind blew around the chimney pots that night
And the rain splashed over the gutters
In the distance a light shone on the horizon

And
As I waited patiently
The light grew brighter
Illuminating a path to be trod with hope, eagerness and adventure

And
Knowing the journey of my soul
Before the light blinded me
I set off on that journey

And
My soul smiled knowingly[5]

"Faithfully" (for Tor)

Faithfully
I followed the journey of my ancestors
Not just my life
But theirs
Has led to this place

Faithfully
I paused on the high plateau
And gazed

Faithfully
I gazed at the journey to now

Faithfully
I gazed at the journey from now
And at all the smiling faces of those who too had journeyed here
From their different places

Faithfully and quietly
We set off together[6]

PERSONAL ENCOUNTER 6.3 – JOHN CAMPBELL AND MY COLLEAGUES AT PRIMEAST: "START WITH THE END IN MIND" (COVEY)

I met John as I was preparing to speak at a conference for the Confederation of British Industry (CBI) in 2001, a year after I had set up my own business. John was also preparing to speak at the same conference and invited me to the Primeast office to meet and compare notes.

I thoroughly enjoyed meeting John and the rest of his team and speaking at the CBI conference. Soon after that, John asked me to lead some client work as an associate. This went well and, in February 2002, I was invited to join the board of Primeast as managing director.

I enjoyed immensely working with the founding directors including John, Gary Edwards (now CEO) and Warwick Abbott. I helped grow the board and practitioner team by inviting Russell Evans (my successor at the helm), Sarah Cave and Martin Carver to join us, together with Simon Tarver (invited by Gary). This core team has been the driving force for most of my time with Primeast and is now supplemented by new energy from directors Emma Heaps and Sarah Morgan.

My reason for mentioning this wonderful team of people, as well as everyone else in the business and our associates around the world, is to acknowledge the immense wisdom I have been blessed to work with for almost half my working life.

John's compassionate leadership and personal conviction to make the world a better place have prevailed even to this day, long after his retirement. His focus on "outcomes" for every client intervention and to "start with that end in mind" (gleaned from Steven Covey) is a simple and profound wisdom that thwarts any temptation to react. Many of our client interventions have been tough and testing (of them and of us as practitioners). We have worked collaboratively with them and (although we wouldn't have always expressed it as such) in service of a defined "brighter future".

Much of this team's wisdom has been built into Primeast's values and systems. Simple concepts such as "design verification" – where no programme of work is presented to a client without an appropriate second eye being cast over the design – require humility and openness to critique and improvement. Collaboration at all levels is promoted with such practices as "buddying" – simple one-on-one support that ignores any hint of hierarchy. And, irrespective of business challenges, the way we recognise and celebrate important occasions such as birthdays, births and marriages is woven into the fabric of day-to-day life. The same applies to sadder occasions where I have never witnessed anything other than compassionate leadership.

Just before I stepped down from the board, I recall a deep conversation with my colleagues about the future of the business. Feelings were unanimous, that our purpose was to make the world a better place and continue to build a company that would serve clients and our staff for many years, long after the current directors had moved on.

Although John has been retired for several years now, I (and others) still meet up with him to share his thoughtful take on our world.

Clearly, I have been fortunate to work amongst wise people throughout my career. Not just at Primeast but also in the electricity industry as well. My fear, in this chapter, is that I inevitably omit many wise individuals. They may not all be in this text, but I treasure their influence.

As a special category, I want to mention the wisdom I have gleaned from thought leaders. Because of the nature of my work, I have been able to learn directly or indirectly from some amazing people. People like Richard Barrett, the founder of Barrett Values Centre who kindly wrote the foreword to *Designing the Purposeful World* and Dr Clayton Lafferty, the founder of Human Synergistics.[7] Sadly, Clay died in 1997, just before my trip to Detroit to learn and become accredited in the use of his diagnostics.

So many thought leaders come to mind as I write, and my next encounter is special indeed because of his deep understanding of the challenges we face in the world and his sense of the future.

PERSONAL ENCOUNTER 6.4 – BOB ANDERSON: "THE WISDOM OF BEING AS ONE"

My first encounter with the wisdom of Bob Anderson was when I was introduced to the book *Scaling Leadership* which he co-authored with Bill Adams. I referenced Bob and Bill's amazing work with mangroves in Chapter 3 on Vitality. The thinking behind their book is also the foundation for the Leadership Circle diagnostic which I experienced in 2016 and became a practitioner for in 2019.

The Leadership Circle assesses a leader's Reactive tendencies and Creative competencies, thus providing a powerful route map from being Reactive (which limits our effectiveness) to being Creative (which supports effectiveness).

But that's not the reason I cite Bob in one of my personal encounters with wisdom. Since becoming a practitioner in 2019, I have connected with Bob directly and have been fortunate to have a number of online conversations during which I was struck by his deep and gentle wisdom.

Bob knows from first-hand experience that our journeys as leaders have potential that vastly exceeds being Creative. Indeed, the journey from being Creative through Integral leadership to Unity is well documented for those interested. And, for me, our wisdom lies within our ability to first glimpse and then embrace Unity.

126 What is *beyond* sustainability? The six aspirations

In Bob's white paper "The Future of Leadership Is Integral Informed by Unity",[8] he explains the need for what I would call wisdom which he references as "Integral informed by Unity" – which is an excellent way of describing the need:

> The world has become exponentially more complex. Our organizations are stretched and strained by the complex forces emerging on all fronts. Covid persists. As office space reopens, employees are choosing to work from home. Talent acquisition and retention is challenging with "The Great Resignation". Global supply chains are severely constrained, and inflation is rearing its ugly head. In the leadership vernacular, VUCA (Volatility, Uncertainty, Complexity, Ambiguity) has been augmented by BANI (Brittle, Anxious, Non-linear, and Incomprehensible).
>
> And if that were not enough, at the time of this writing, climate scientists have published the direst report yet, and Russia is waging a brutal war on Ukraine. The foundations of our current order of civilization are shaking – if not imploding. Back to normal is not an option. It is a death sentence. This moment in planetary history calls us to create a new, higher order of society.
>
> Our future depends on how we rise to this moment. The leadership challenge before us is not merely managing through turbulent times. We are challenged with rightening civilization. As leaders, we must navigate VUCA/BANI and, as we do, position our organizations to contribute to a new and thriving planetary future. This puts an unprecedented demand on the accelerated development of highly conscious and effective leaders at every level of the organization.

Later in the same white paper, Bob describes the essence of Unity consciousness:

> I am not the body, nor the mind. I am not separate, but one with the inherent unity of all things". We ecstatically realize the obvious and astonishing unity underlying diversity – the oneness of all things with itself. This is the birth of universal compassion, "I am my brother and my sister. We are all each other! The earth and all beings are one life.

My brief encounters with Bob have been too few and too brief. I know there will be more to follow, and I eagerly await the adventures in wisdom that we will share in the years to come.

Profound wisdom **127**

I've saved my final personal encounter with wisdom for my Mum, affectionately known to her grandchildren and great-grandchildren as simply "Granny".

PERSONAL ENCOUNTER 6.5 – MARGARET WILSON: "GRANNY'S CAFÉ"

I suppose I should confess that my biological mother, Sally Wilson, died shortly after my birth. She actually never left hospital since the day she brought me into the world. So, I don't remember anything about her, except a felt-sense that she loved me very much.

Just after I was born, my Dad had to leave the UK to work in Canada. He was away for four years, during which time I was well cared for by my Auntie Pat and Uncle Sid and their already five boys. I was the sixth. It was great having five "brothers". But equally great when my Dad returned with my "new Mum".

At four years old I moved in with them and soon was joined with a new younger sister, Lynne. We grew happily as a family, and I never stopped to think of Margaret as anything other than "Mum".

Mum was a teacher at the same primary school in Leeds that I attended as a child. In fact, due to a quirk of age, I actually spent my last two years there in her class. She treated me just like any of the other children, except, if I was really naughty, in which case I'd be in bother with my Dad when I got home.

The summer holidays of 1966 fell between junior and senior school for me. I was on holiday with our family. We'd had a lovely day out at Robin Hood's Bay on the Yorkshire Coast, and I remember commenting how fortunate I was to have such wonderful parents. From the back seat of our Ford Anglia where I was sitting next to Lynne, I noticed my Mum and Dad looking at each other.

They sensed that the time was right to tell me about my biological Mum. I forget my exact words, but I said how grateful I was that they shared my history, and I also affirmed that I still had the best Mum and Dad in the world.

At the time of writing, my Mum is 96 years old. My Dad passed away over ten years ago, and Mum still lives on her own in the house where I grew up. She is always really positive and cheerful. She has

128 What is *beyond* sustainability? The six aspirations

less mobility now but manages with the help of a stairlift and various mobility aids.

Her subtle wisdom takes the form of total non-judgement and an amazing ability to listen to her family members who bring her no end of challenges. She doesn't try to solve them all and she usually manages to stay calm and positive. I usually pop over on a Sunday with a meal that we share together in what I call "Granny's café".

As well as her family, Mum's legacy includes thousands of others who passed through her various classes at the schools she served. Many are still in touch – a testimony to her wise guidance and skilful teaching.

Perhaps you too have friends or family members who you visit from time to time and benefit from their wisdom. I hope this encounter of mine encourages you to acknowledge the support you receive from special others in your own life.

Chapter summary

Who are the individuals or organisations you know of who are actively supporting the growth of wisdom in our world?

Make a note of your top six (notice), preferably those where you have some kind of personal connection. Check them out online and post a suitable case study of your own on social media (celebrate) with your own words of encouragement. If you're struggling (which I doubt very much) then check out some of the cases in this chapter and simply post their work online.

And what about you? Make a note of six things you're already doing to facilitate growth of wisdom – either for yourself or for others. Then make a note of six more things you'd like to do in the future – preferably in your diary on the date you're going to make a start.

We'll return to Wisdom again later in the book

Because Wisdom is such a vital aspiration for our brighter future, we return to it again in Part III as we explore the subject a little deeper and offer the "Wisdom Code" as an opportunity to contemplate what it is that makes us wise and, from this data, form a plan to accelerate the development of our wisdom.

Notes

1 Wilson C. A. 2024. Poem "Wisdom" by Author.
2 Actualized, 2017. Leo Gura: https://youtu.be/wa-NAtBEMkA?si=GczChkX0 lRT-GvYe
3 Barrett, R. 2020. *Worldview Dynamics and the Well-Being of Nations*: www.barrett academy.com/books/world-view-dynamics-and-the-well-being-of-nations
4 Barrett Values Centre 2024. Barrett Values Centre – "seven levels" model: www. valuescentre.com/
5 Wilson, C. A. 2024. Poem "And" by Author.
6 Wilson, C. A. 2024. Poem "Faithfully" by Author.
7 Human Synergistics International, 2024. Human Synergistics: www.humans ynergistics.com/
8 Anderson, R. J. 2022. "The Future of Leadership Is Integral Informed by Unity": https://leadershipcircle.com/wp-content/uploads/2022/10/Future-of-Leadership-Integral-In-formed-by-Unity.pdf

Part II

Leading a diverse team of players

A role for everyone 7

Twelve archetypes

Awesome folk

My I've met some awesome folk
People with energy
With dreams that have to be
With indignation that must play out
With the power
If they knew it
To change the universe
Blummin' 'eck just do it

Theirs is the future
The future for our children
In their hands
In their hearts
And in their minds

They already do so much
And with discernment
And courage
Their dreams
And outrage
Their impact could be magnified
By listening
To what's inside

DOI: 10.4324/9781003428121-10

134 Leading a diverse team of players

By asking why?
Ah yes
I get all that but why?

Is a mountain for the climbing
Just because it's there?
Or is there something else
Calling?
Is it worth a prayer?
A moment's silence
Again to ask why?

Sometimes the things we do for adventure
Have more meaning than we know

Do we fly to space to walk on the moon?
Or to gaze back at our world?

Do we step into the ocean to swim?
Or to feel the might and wonderful balance
Of our world?
Our precious world?

I've met some awesome folk
And they're discovering
Why
Why they're awesome
And why the mountain must be climbed[1]

Elvis Presley made our differences clear when he sang these words adapted from William Shakespeare's play "As you like it": "You know someone said that the world's a stage and each of us must play a part". We explore the parts we play and how we can engage constructively in this part of the book.

In Part I of this book, we made quite a bit of progress. We affirmed the benefits of aiming beyond the challenge of sustainability to the kind of world we'd all like to see for future generations. We explored some reasons for hope and confidence. Part of this is understanding the mathematics of complexity regarding humanity's response to any situation. In a nutshell,

A role for everyone: Twelve archetypes **135**

there are billions of people looking at the challenges and opportunities we face from a plethora of different perspectives according to their situation and sense of their own capability. And, because of our diversity and spread, the "system" simply works.

That said, we need to recognise the criticality of this moment in time. We have reached a place where our brighter future is definitely within reach, and many commentators absolutely believe we can and will deliver it. However, and for good reason, others fear that the situation is dire and leaders are not treating it as seriously as they could and should. The challenge with this is that people become entrenched with others who think as they do. Consequently, society becomes polarised in its views, and we spend more time fighting than we do taking positive action. Our "system" could work even better if we consciously pulled together.

My encouragement to everyone reading this book is to become a "curious encourager". We do well to be curious in the full spectrum of views that matter to us – not just the ones that align with our personal stance. This book is called *Leading Beyond Sustainability* for a reason. Every single one of us has the opportunity to show leadership to those around us and, in today's world, effective leadership is not about forcing our views on others who may disagree. It is about having wise, respectful conversations, characterised by a spirit of curiosity and collaboration. The more we explore, the more we learn. The more we learn, the more we are able to speak and act in a helpful way.

This part of the book focuses on these vital issues. It encourages us to seek to understand others and to remain positive, constructive and creative.

Twelve characters for six aspirations

In Part I, I described our "better world" using six aspirations: connection, peace, vitality, abundance, opportunity and wisdom. And, just as there are six aspirations to achieve, there is a range of character types at play in their delivery.

I got to thinking about some of the key characters involved in this system – amazing people all with different perspectives and abilities. My list is not definitive. I'm sure you can think of other characters at play. To serve our thought process and keep the conversation simple, I've created 12 of these characters as follows (Figure 7.1):

136 Leading a diverse team of players

Character	Statement	Marks/10	Total
INNOVATOR	I am progressing great ideas to make the world a better place		
	I am contributing my creativity to industry in support of a brighter future		
	I know better ways to do things that can solve the problems of our age		
SPECIALIST	I have skills, knowledge and resources that can help improve the world		
	I shall focus my efforts on the part of the problem I'm best equipped for		
	I am constantly equipping myself to play an important role for the world		
CONNECTOR	I frequently put people in touch with others to improve our world		
	I know many people who are making the world a much better place		
	I enjoy meeting people who are working hard for our environment		
FACILITATOR	I find ways to support people who are improving our world		
	I provide opportunities for people to find ways to make our future brighter		
	I organise events about securing a better world for future generations		
ACTIVIST	I speak out against actions that will harm our world		
	I participate in group action in support of a better world		
	I don't mind if my action for a better world is unpopular – I'll still take it		
EVANGELIST	I want to share my ideas on making the world a better place		
	I take time to connect widely in order to focus people on a better world		
	I speak passionately about the benefits of sustainability		
OPTIMIST	I am certain we will find a way to a better and more sustainable future		
	Humanity has massive potential to solve the problems we face		
	I am amazed by the fabulous work being done to secure a better future		
EXPLORER	Whenever I notice news about sustainability, I take great interest		
	I like to understand the challenges we face and what can be done		
	A great deal of my learning is dedicated to exploring a better future		
ENCOURAGER	When I hear about progress towards a brighter future, I share the news		
	I offer enthusiastic encouragement to those working for a better future		
	I invest significant time and money with those pursuing a better world		
APATHIST	I have more important things to worry about than the future of our world		
	Other people can look after the future		
	I really don't care about the long term, I'm enjoying today		
DENIER	There is no problem with the future, the world is fine as it is		
	The whole sustainability thing is a conspiracy theory		
	The world is changing, irrespective of what humans do		
SABOTEUR	I have too much to lose from the status quo, I'll tell the opposite story		
	For every idea in favour of the green agenda, I shall give two against it		
	I frequently speak out against sustainability and the green agenda		

Figure 7.1 Twelve characters for six aspirations.

A role for everyone: Twelve archetypes **137**

a. Innovator
b. Specialist
c. Connector
d. Facilitator
e. Activist
f. Evangelist
g. Optimist
h. Explorer
i. Encourager
j. Apathist
k. Denier
l. Saboteur

ACTIVITY

To help you determine your own characteristics as a "leader beyond sustainability", consider the statements in Figure 7.1. Mark each statement out of ten where ten is "absolutely" and zero is "not at all". Add up the points out of 30 for each character and rank the characters in order. Hopefully, this will give you an informed sense of who you are in this quest for a brighter future.

Note that Apathist can be regarded as neutral to the cause and Denier and Saboteur as negative. But, as we shall see later, they still have a role to play.

Once again, I remind you that this is not an exact science. There are many more personalities at work in our quest for paradise than could possibly be described in a brief narrative. But I've tested this with friends, colleagues and attendees at workshops – and I believe this is a pretty good mix. Twelve is a good number to work with, and I'm sure most of us will see ourselves in some combination of the 12.

Whilst nine characters are clearly positive, note that there is one that could be regarded as neutral and a couple that many people would see as negative. This reflects a belief that, overall, the positive contributors outnumber the others, certainly in terms of their effectiveness. However, all these characters have a part to play – even if it's only to raise the game of the others by testing their perspective. Well, that's my view for what it's worth.

Let's now get to know the characters a little better before giving you a chance to finally decide how you and those you know fit in (Figure 7.2).

138 Leading a diverse team of players

Figure 7.2 What kind of environmentalist are you?

Innovator

For every challenge, there is a solution and innovators are all around us. They may have their own great ideas or even take the creativity of others and turn it into something practical for the advancement of mankind and the world we inhabit.

Specialist

These people have spent significant time understanding subjects and turning their talents into clear strengths to benefit us all. Sometimes they are so focused on their own specialisms that they might not understand the bigger picture.

Connector

And so we have connectors. They join the dots; they connect people with other people and organisations to organisations. They build teams,

A role for everyone: Twelve archetypes **139**

corporations, institutions, governments and more. They may even be the connectors of ideas, taking the innovators to new levels.

Facilitator

These people weave their magic to make things happen. They trust that the knowledge is "in the room" or "in the community", and they offer processes to draw it out and turn it into action. They may not be the ones doing the doing but often the doing isn't done without them.

Activist

Not content to let nature take care of things, the activists are on the front line. They provide a sense of urgency and stir up the "powers that be". They are often willing to put themselves on a pedestal or even in danger to support what they see as an important cause.

Evangelist

Evangelists are certain of the way forward and want to share their message with confidence and conviction. They delight in finding new platforms and channels for their message. They want to be heard and to enlist others to join them in their quest.

Optimist

The optimists are confident that solutions can be found and that a brighter future is there for the taking. They see challenges as opportunities for progress. As for failure, well there's no such thing – each setback is simply a learning opportunity.

Explorer

Explorers are curious. If they don't know the answer to the problem, they will find it – in a book, online or through their network. Their journey will

140 Leading a diverse team of players

take them on many adventures, pushing back the boundaries of knowledge as they go.

Encourager

Every time we notice, encourage and celebrate someone who is changing the world, we are changing the world (where have we heard that before?). Encouragers give the rest of us the strength, energy and commitment to go that extra mile.

Apathist

You're probably thinking that these people are not the ones we need on our journey to a brighter future. But let's think about it. They may be in our team or organisation already and perhaps they are just waiting to be fired up and pointed in the right direction. They are also a valuable source to test the rigour and validity of our message. When we answer their awkward questions, we strengthen our resolve. And we might just move them to a more constructive stance.

Denier

One of two potentially negative characters, these players will suggest that our quest isn't necessary. There is simply no problem to solve. And they may be very articulate and convincing. But they have their uses. They require that the rest of us check our facts, present our case well and provide better arguments to deliver the brighter future we seek.

Saboteur

Last but by no means least, saboteurs seem to be fighting the battle for the other side. But they might still be on our team or in our business. Either way, they seek to take the wind from our sails to serve their own interests or alternative beliefs. However, as with deniers, they present an opportunity for us to provide a strong case for change that hopefully will convince them or at least persuade others in the dialogue. Indeed, it's worth remembering

A role for everyone: Twelve archetypes **141**

that they may have a point. Through dialogue, it might simply be one part of our own belief system that is flawed. As we listen to them, we might grow to see at least some of their perspective, and they might begin to see some of ours.

ACTIVITY

So, having completed the previous activity and read the above brief descriptions, how would you describe your own character? Do you fit neatly into one of the above descriptions or perhaps you're a combination of two, three or even more? Make a note of your thoughts in your journal.

I think I'm probably an optimistic facilitator and encourager. People who know me well will doubtless let me know.

ACTIVITY

The second thing I'd like you to think about is how you regard the other characters. I have a hunch you might have little regard for some. Does this mean you ignore them? What if you actively sought them out and encouraged them to share their story whilst you listen without judgement?

Note your thoughts in your journal.

Characters involved in the case studies and "personal encounters" in Part I of this book

Which of the characters mentioned in Part I of this book inspired you the most? From the brief narratives and the general impressions you formed of them, what characteristics from this chapter apply to them?

Have you noticed any tendency you might have to be drawn to the stories you most relate to or judge to be more important than others?

142 Leading a diverse team of players

People we admire and those we don't

What about people you admire for the impact they're having on the world? Again, whose work resonates with you? And who do you know who is really working hard to make the world a better place – but perhaps not in a way that resonates with you? What if you spent a little time trying to understand their perspective and passion for what they do?

These days, I find myself getting to know people I meet. What do they do? Why do they do it? What is their story that led them to now? Where is all this heading?

I am noticing that, more and more, these conversations result in me thanking them for making the world a better place. We need such a variety of creative people to make the world amazing and so often we take them for granted.

Note

1 Wilson, C. A. 2022. Poem "Awesome Folk" by Author.

Who are you and how do you relate to others? 8

Once we understand the roles each of us play in delivering a brighter future, the next big question is how we regard, connect and collaborate with others. This is true in any aspect of our lives, and especially in our working lives. For organisations, there will probably be a diverse mix of characters in the workforce. Understanding the mix and making use of this diversity is key to making progress. Even those with opposite views or characteristics to our own can be immensely helpful in understanding their stance and perhaps helping each other to learn.

Note that, as humans, we may tend to associate with and discuss our work with people who have similar characteristics to our own. This can cause cliques and silos in our workplace or community. Instead, we might wish to consider the merit of meaningful conversation with people who see the world differently from ourselves.

Our tendency to judge

In 2012, Shirzad Chamine published his book *Positive Intelligence:*[1] *Why Only 20% of Teams and Individuals Achieve Their True Potential and How You Can Achieve Yours*. Alongside this thought-provoking book, his team provides an excellent set of diagnostics and learning resources to support growth in Positive Intelligence. In 2022, most of the practitioner team at Primeast participated in a "PQ" learning programme and worked together in small cohorts to practice new techniques and behaviours. Every one of us found

DOI: 10.4324/9781003428121-11

144 Leading a diverse team of players

this development helpful and pertinent to our work as leadership coaches and facilitators.

I personally made the link between positivity and sustainability, and this was a contributory nudge to me writing this book.

Shirzad beautifully characterises the traits of humans in two main categories, *Sages* and *Saboteurs*. Sages, as the name suggests, *act* with wisdom and positivity, whereas Saboteurs tend to *react* with negativity, thwarting our good intentions, confidence and performance. I say there are two main categories because the Saboteurs take a variety of different forms (please do check out the book or Shirzad's plethora of online resources). But the "Chief Saboteur" is *The Judge*. This is so relevant to this chapter in the ways listed below.

Judging ourselves

Many of us have a tendency to judge ourselves – and often quite harshly. Maybe we compare our sense of self with others' expectations, perhaps it was our parents, teachers, friends, colleagues, boss and so on. Or maybe, in this age of social media we compare our sense of self with the carefully edited persona of others as portrayed online. Or maybe we overfocus on our failures and less on our many successes. Shirzad encourages us to revisit our sense of self and "fall in love" with who we really are at our essence.

Judging others

Not surprisingly, we also have a tendency to judge others. Do we like them? Do we align with their thinking? Do we respect their stance on topics we care about? And, in judging others, do we tend to draw closer to them or distance ourselves? Again, Shirzad encourages us to see the best in others and respect them for who they are.

Judging situations

Father Edward J. Flanagan, the founder of Boys Town, proclaimed there was "no such thing as a bad boy, only bad environment, bad modeling, and bad teaching".[2] A variation (or perhaps extension) to this theme is the thought that "there is no such thing as a bad circumstance, just a poor (or unwise) response to it". We learn from both these thoughts that judging circumstances as bad in their essence is unhelpful. A better stance is to consider each circumstance as a given and consider what opportunities it presents. This is also part of the teaching of Positive Intelligence (or PQ).

Pertinent to this book we might understandably judge climate change to be a bad circumstance. And we might equally be tempted to judge and blame others for their part in its cause, but is this the most helpful stance? What merit is there instead in looking for the plethora of opportunities to take advantage of technologies such as renewable energy, electric and autonomous transport and meat from precision fermentation (just to name a few) to give us a cleaner, healthier world and fabulous opportunity to rewild our countryside and oceans at the same time. Even if climate change hadn't been the enormous challenge that it clearly is, wouldn't these be great things to do anyway?

Alternative strategies to judgement

It's really hard to refrain from judging ourselves, others and circumstances. It takes a great deal of mindfulness, self-control, tolerance and positive attitude. As we discussed in Chapter 6, this comes with a growth in our personal and collective Wisdom, which is one reason why I named it as one of just six aspirations for our brighter future. It is also the reason why I have chosen Wisdom as the theme to focus on in Part III of this book. How much progress could we make if an ever-increasing number of people kept an open mind and always looked for positive change without condemning our current circumstances or the actions of those that brought us here?

Judgement, as described in *Positive Intelligence*, is harsh, blame-orientated and debilitating. But that is not to say that we shouldn't respond to the evidence of our circumstances. Although *Judgement* and *Discernment* are words oft-used interchangeably, I like to focus on (my sense of) the differences. Discernment considers the evidence of our circumstances and the knowledge and tools available to make positive change. Discernment helps us to articulate the reasons for change, and Wisdom helps us to explore the options before diving in. To me, *Judgement* prompts *reaction* whereas *Discernment* prompts *creative action*, taking account of our longer-term vision.

146 Leading a diverse team of players

Discernment informed by rationality

Earlier in this book, I referenced the work of Steven Pinker, especially his book *Rationality*.[3] Pinker's thesis is essentially that we should avoid being dismayed by over-focusing on news headlines as they tend to amplify what is going wrong in the world. It is unsurprising that doing so tends to make us *judge* our circumstances as adverse and may make us pessimistic regarding our future. Instead, his work provides encouragement to check out the data and the trends regarding the issues we care about. Doing so will often reassure us that people are living longer, better educated, healthier, more fulfilled, wealthier and more peaceful than ever before. Of course, that's not to say that these benefits are evenly spread across humanity or that there aren't blips in the data. But I find the more I look, the more I am reassured that hopeful prospects are improving at a blistering pace.

Pinker affirms that checking the data and being reassured in this way is not optimism. He suggests that optimism is an unfounded belief in a brighter future without the evidence to support it. Checking the data and being guided by it is rationalism, and I propose the following:

diligent rationalism informs our discernment

The motive for this is not simply to give us a "feel good" factor, though feeling good is a healthy way to be. What really matters, in my mind, is to research beneath the data, to understand what happened to cause an improvement and build on it.

When Elon Musk made his patents for electric vehicles and batteries open-source, he did so not because he was naïve to competition but because he realised what it would take to disrupt the internal combustion engine industry and knew this could be accelerated through sharing. This attitude is a rational, discerning, creative response (I choose my words carefully) and so valuable in mitigating climate change and in any other change we wish to make.

This is the spirit of our fourth aspiration, Abundance. Our gorgeous planet and space beyond it provide enough of everything we need for joyful living and the nurturing of a fabulous world for all of life. We simply and progressively need to discern and consciously choose appropriate technologies, systems, processes and behaviours to access all that everyone needs.

It seems to me that a key enabler of the brighter future we all want is keeping our attitude positive. I stress that this is not about living with false hope in a fool's paradise. This is not optimism. It is not pessimism; it is discerning rationalism blended with positivity.

ACTIVITY

Thought experiment: should we conserve our planet's resources, limit energy consumption, stop travelling and stop eating meat? Or should we deploy and count on the latest technology to solve the climate crisis?

Before progressing, make some notes in your journal on your stance, having read this book this far.

In his book *Brighter* (mentioned earlier), Adam Dorr makes a compelling case for maintaining a prosperous society so that we have the funds to invest in the changes that will take us to a world where we can consciously regulate carbon dioxide and other greenhouse gases. He also suggests that appropriate change is happening at breakneck speed, driven initially by a will to change but, most importantly, by economics. In a nutshell, clean, cheap, renewable energy, autonomous electric transport as a service (TaaS), meat from precision fermentation (requiring no slaughtered animals and freeing up pasture the area of three continents for rewilding) and massively reduced labour costs due to artificial intelligence will have the effect of, first of all, slowing climate change and then reversing it.

Here speaks the optimistic, specialist innovator. Dorr's argument is so compelling and I confess to my admiration of him and the team at RethinkX. But does it mean that I think the other players in the climate debate are wrong? What about the activists? Greta Thunberg, David Attenborough, Extinction Rebellion and Just Stop Oil (in their different ways) are passionate advocates of cutting emissions by doing less. Are they wrong in their stance and actions? What about the millions of people who have deployed new technology simply because they consider it the right thing to do?

My sense of all this is to accept that it is this rich mix of different perspectives, the playing out of the different characters I introduced above that will take us to our brighter future. If well-intentioned people take stock of their world as they see it and choose a course of action, who are we to judge them?

148 Leading a diverse team of players

That is not to say that there shouldn't be challenges along the path. Taking time to listen and discuss different potential solutions with people who are different from ourselves is often the key missing ingredient to the progress we seek.

I would encourage every reader of this book and those we consequently engage with to keep an open mind to solutions for climate change and all the other changes we wish to see and to enter into constructive dialogue with other parties. We should, first of all, listen and then ask questions to help deepen our understanding of their perspective. Then, we can politely ask the other person if they'd be happy to hear our own perspective and to ask questions to deepen their understanding. Such a conversation, if carried out in a spirit of learning, may well result in both parties taking action, maybe in order to answer questions they couldn't respond to at the time, perhaps to share articles or other references that explain a relevant topic, and perhaps to act on something that came up in conversation that we didn't know.

I cannot overemphasise how much this approach is part of *Leading Beyond Sustainability*. In a simple conversation of perhaps an hour or so, two people can come together in a spirit of good intention, understanding and learning. Sometimes such conversations culminate in no shift of stance from either party. However, my personal experience is that, if the conversation is managed well, both parties will indeed learn something. If we are the party that has learnt, again, I cannot overemphasise how powerful it is to thank the other party for sharing something we weren't previously aware of.

As I mentioned above, in the context of *Positive Intelligence*, Judgement prompts *reaction* whereas Discernment prompts *creative action*. There is nothing more powerful to help leaders to distinguish between *reactive tendencies* and *creative competencies* than the book *Scaling Leadership* by Bob Anderson (who I introduced in Chapter 6) and his co-author and co-founder Bill Adams. Their Leadership Circle diagnostic makes this very clear as you can discover for yourself in the following activity.

ACTIVITY

Take a look at the website of Leadership Circle.[4] Look at the Leadership Assessment Tools that are on offer there. Take a look at the Leadership Circle Profile and maybe even take the free self-assessment (assuming it is still available when you read this book). Either way, read or listen

> to any narrative on the difference between Creative Competences and Reactive Tendencies.
>
> My question to you, the reader, is this:
>
> In your own words, to what extent do these characteristics play out in our quest to create a better world?
>
> Make notes in your journal.

How do we listen to others?

I've hinted above that Listening is a key Wisdom skill. It is so important in our quest for a brighter future that I feel compelled to offer further comment. When we listen and refrain from judgement, we become more inclined to engage and hear new perspectives on a particular topic or circumstance. We might therefore want to pay particular attention to the quality of listening we adopt during conversations, especially with people different to ourselves.

Otto Scharmer, author of *Theory U*, describes four levels of listening with ascending effectiveness (I paraphrase):

1. **CLOSED MIND:** We listen to hear information that supports our own view of the world.
2. **OPEN MIND:** We listen to hear and learn from new information, even if it is contra to our firmly held worldview.
3. **OPEN HEART:** We listen for new information and in such a way that we notice and respond to the feelings of those we are in dialogue with. This provides much more information than simply facts.
4. **GENERATIVE LISTENING:** We listen with an open mind, an open heart and with a curious attention to the brighter future (at any scale) that is being facilitated by the conversation and which is aligned to a brighter future for all humanity.

ACTIVITY

Arrange a meeting with a group of people with whom you share a common interest or cause. It could be a team from your organisation, a community group, a project team, the local branch of your professional institute or even your family.

150 Leading a diverse team of players

Ask each person to consider the 12 characters listed in the previous chapter and choose up to three descriptions that most apply to them. Share these attributes within the group and ask people to choose one or two people who are clearly different characters to themselves.

Ask them to take time (say half-an-hour) to have a conversation about their work and the brighter future they would like to see.

In a plenary share what people have learnt – and make notes in your journal.

Notes

1 Chamine, S. 2012. *Positive Intelligence*: www.positiveintelligence.com/
2 Wikipedia, 2024. Edward J Flanagan: https://en.wikipedia.org/wiki/Edward_J._Flanagan
3 Pinker, S. 2022. *Rationality*: https://stevenpinker.com/publications/rationality-what-it-why-it-seems-so-scarce-and-why-it-matters
4 Linked In, 2024. Leadership Circle: https://leadershipcircle.com/

Leading the action   9

This chapter is one of reflection and action. At this stage, I want leaders to fully appreciate the immense good they and those they know are probably already doing to deliver a better world. We will offer a threefold response that anyone can make which serves us well. It is embodied in the following phrase:

> *Every time we notice, encourage and celebrate someone who is changing the world, we are changing the world.*

I encourage you as readers and leaders to take stock of your most valuable insights from the book so far and to consider the action you need to take in order to be part of the evolving future. This is a brighter future that is happening, our quest is to determine to what extent we wish to accelerate it and help it on its way. In Parts III and IV, we will build on these insights to closely examine the importance of Wisdom (beyond our thoughts in Chapter 6) and the power of Alignment, taking us back to where my thinking in Purposeful Leadership began.

Reflecting on Part I of this book

Part I comprises six chapters each relating to one of our six aspirations for a better world. In each chapter, I recount some of my *Personal Encounters* with people and organisations who are contributing to a brighter future for humanity and this gorgeous planet we call home.

DOI: 10.4324/9781003428121-12

152 Leading a diverse team of players

These are just a few of many people whose endeavours I have *noticed*. In my own way, I have tried to encourage them in their work and by referencing them in this book I am, again in my own way, celebrating what they do.

> ## ACTIVITY
>
> Stop for a moment and make a list in your journal of people who have significantly noticed, encouraged and celebrated what you do.

When I did this activity, I noted some candidates you might expect: my parents; my wife Frances; my children; curiously only four teachers from all my time at school (one of whom was my mother who had the dubious delight of teaching me for my last two years at primary school); a handful of bosses (not all of them); a few colleagues, associates and clients; and an even smaller number of friends. Yes, there were others who thanked me for a job well done but, on reflection, the number of people offering sincere and significant encouragement and taking the time to truly celebrate what I do is small in comparison to the vast number of people I have engaged with in my life.

Let me be authentic and frank. This is not a complaint. I don't do the work I do for recognition or gratitude. I do it because I hope it makes a difference. I know it does, because of the people I have worked with who fed back to me that what we worked on together changed their lives or improved their business in some significant way. I'm not looking for sympathy either. I'm trying to name an uncomfortable truth that most of us fail most of the time to notice, encourage and celebrate the work of others to make our world a brighter place, myself included.

I've also noticed that the more we do it, or should I say "the more I do it", it becomes a positive habit.

In fact, this book would never have been published by Routledge if it hadn't been for one of my encouraging colleagues.

Thank you Russell

I met Russell Evans[1] in 2004 when he contacted me at Primeast enquiring about the work we did and wanting to discuss his own career going forward. We met up for a coffee in Harrogate and talked for ages. I was impressed

Leading the action   **153**

by his positivity, enthusiasm and obvious interpersonal skills. I know this sounds strange but on this very first meeting, I felt sure I had found a successor to me to run our consulting business beyond 2008 which was the timestamp for the vision my colleagues and I were working towards delivering.

We engaged Russell as an associate, working on contracts to deliver client assignments, then as an employed Senior Consultant, then as a Board Director. Russell exceeded my expectations and, as 2008 approached, our board approved my suggestion that he should take the reins of the business.

Russell led the business well through some tough times, including a financial crash and a global pandemic, both of which seriously disrupted our industry. Despite these challenges, he presided over significant business growth in terms of talent, revenue, scale, global reach, portfolio and winning two prestigious Queens Awards for Enterprise in 2015 and 2021 in the process. He continued until 2023 when he, in turn, passed the reins to one of our founding directors, Gary Edwards.[2]

An early indication of Russell's ability to notice, encourage and celebrate my own work was regarding our PrimeFocus framework, something I had personally developed and used frequently in client assignments to help senior leadership teams align to a powerful purpose. Russell showed a high level of curiosity to know more about my thinking behind the model. He joined me in several conference "tours" in Europe, the United States and Africa and consequently encouraged me to seek a publisher (Kogan Page) for *Designing the Purposeful Organization* and its sequel *Designing the Purposeful World* (Routledge).

In 2022, I shared with Russell my thoughts about *Leading Beyond Sustainability* and my intention to self-publish the book. Russell was adamant that the thinking was "seminal" and that self-publishing was not the route to go. Shortly after our walk, I had a conversation with my previous publishing editor at Routledge, and we quickly signed a contract to write this book.

The purpose of me telling this story is not to share my journey, rather it is to celebrate Russell's rare ability to inspire the efforts of people around him. Without his unceasing encouragement, my professional life would have been very different. This is the power of these three words: notice, encourage and celebrate.

So, coming back to your list, whose encouragement are you grateful for and how have you expressed your gratitude? Is there more you need to do?

154 Leading a diverse team of players

It's never too late

If you're anything like me, when you completed your list of people who encouraged you, you probably looked at it with a sense of missed opportunity. Perhaps you lost touch with them or perhaps they're no longer alive. Either way, we both probably neglected to show our gratitude in the most meaningful way. Of course, if we are in touch or can get in touch, perhaps there's still a chance to say, "thank you". Or maybe there's the possibility to acknowledge it to their friends and family.

Pay it forward

And there is another way. If we're unable to show gratitude to those who noticed, encouraged and celebrated our efforts, we can always multiply that flow of energy (for that is what encouragement is) by consciously acting this way in support of others.

In Part I of this book, I encouraged you in my *Power of Six* exercise to make a note of six people who are working hard (knowingly or otherwise) to deliver one or more of our six aspirations for a brighter future. I wish you success in your further encouragement and celebration of their work. By the way, you have clearly already *noticed* it or you couldn't have added them to your list.

And then there's you

It might sound unnecessary or self-indulgent to notice, encourage and celebrate your own work and that of your business and those working to deliver it. However, my experience suggests that this is where most people (and especially businesses) fail in a big way.

NOTICING – what we do, why we do it and taking stock of our impact

There's more to noticing than meets the eye. Most of us know what we do, but my suggestion is that very few of us have intimate knowledge of why we do it. To bring this to life, check out Simon Sinek's brief but inspiring video "The Golden Circle" on YouTube. Simon encourages us that why we do what we do is way more important than what we do or indeed how we do it. Taking time to really understand and thereby notice our why is one of the most powerful things we can do. You probably picked this up as you read my Personal Encounters stories in Part I.

Then there's noticing our impact. It seems weird, but when I ask business leaders to quantify the financial health of their business, most of them have a really good handle on sales, turnover, profit and loss, net assets, cashflow and so on. When I ask them to similarly describe and quantify the impact their business has, the number that can do this with any degree of confidence or certainty is much smaller. Wouldn't it be impressive if a teacher could say they had taught over a thousand young people during their careers and could say with some confidence how many were happily contributing positively to a brighter future and broadly in which professions, perhaps naming at least a handful of examples?

Think about the work of the team at Poppleton, described in Part I. How many hospitals and pharmaceutical laboratories have their ventilation systems been installed in and how many patients have experienced better health as a consequence? They may know the answer. And if they do, are they using such insights to motivate their workforce and other stakeholders?

ACTIVITY

Almost every person and every business under the sun is working towards a brighter future that matches one or more of the six aspirations. What about you? Which of the six aspirations are you moving the world closer to? Remember, this applies at any level and in every circumstance.

We need to fully take account, for example, of people like Nick in Chapter 1. Although I told his story as an example of deep Connection, I could equally have told it in testimony of someone working tirelessly to care for the health (Vitality) of one person – his wife Linda.

Go ahead, which of the six aspirations are you most impacting and in what way?

156 Leading a diverse team of players

ENCOURAGING – ourselves and those we work together with

It may seem like a strange concept to think about encouraging ourselves. Indeed, it may seem easier and more generous to encourage the efforts of those we work closely with. But the concept of *notice–encourage–celebrate* needs to work at every level. If we neglect to encourage ourselves, especially if we're receiving little encouragement from others, it's easy to see why we might lose motivation and even give up.

The first step to self-encouragement is to go back to step one – *notice*. It makes absolute sense to frequently ask why we do something. It also makes sense to take stock of the real impact we're having and to align it to one or more of the six aspirations. Knowing that we have succeeded in making the world a better place, even if it is for just one person, or one other sentient being or perhaps a forest or maybe just one tree should be all the encouragement we need.

A second step is to share what we do with others. It may seem conceited to "blow our own trumpet", but keeping our best efforts to ourselves isn't helping the world to evolve. Sharing what we do and why we do it isn't boasting, it's simply one way of offering ourselves in service or as a collaborator for others. It's also a reminder to ourselves.

If we work in a team with others in service of a brighter future, encouraging everyone to encourage each other is a key ingredient for high performance.

CELEBRATING – our own impact and that of others we work with

In a similar vein, self-celebration is not something that comes naturally to most of us. But I would suggest we have a duty to do it – for ourselves, for our team, our business and for the world. The newspapers are very quick to remind us of all the bad things that are happening in the world. There is a real need to balance this with a bit of good news. And we do well to follow the advice of Simon Sinek as mentioned earlier. It's not what we've done or even how we did it. It's why we did it and the consequential impact it has had.

Chapter summary

First a quick recap. I hope you've enjoyed this adventure so far into a brighter future beyond sustainability. I wonder what you thought about the six aspirations I proposed in Part I? Perhaps you would have chosen different labels. Maybe you'd have had more than six, or perhaps fewer? That's OK, remember, these aspirations came from my experience of engaging with thousands of people on the better world they'd like to see. They were also informed by my obsessive research and contemplation on how the world is actually changing.

I'm not proposing these six as the next set of goals for world leaders at the United Nations and I'm not looking to start some kind of movement for us all to join and align to. My key aim is to encourage you, the reader, to contemplate your own brighter future, to describe it in words that inspire you and to share your vision with others that they may also be inspired.

I hope you enjoyed the chapter reviews and my challenge for you is to find six people or organisations who are working hard to deliver the aspiration of each chapter or something akin to it. I hope you've taken the time to notice, encourage and celebrate their work.

I hope you enjoyed the thinking in Part II of the way humanity comes together to make positive change. In what way did you relate to the 12 characters that work in their own ways to influence our brighter future? Which characters manifest in your own personality? Perhaps you have your own labels for these players. Did you consider the characteristics of people you know, maybe in your work team? Perhaps you came together as suggested in the activities? Did you find the courage to listen with an open mind, open heart and an ear to the emerging future to someone whose views were different from your own? And what difference did that make?

So, what's next? Introducing Parts III and IV of this book

Writing Parts I and II of this book have been a joy. It has enabled me to have profound clarity about the world I'd like to see and work towards. It has made me appreciate the millions of people and organisations who are already making this happen. I am more inclined than ever to notice, encourage and celebrate those who are taking us to a brighter future.

158 Leading a diverse team of players

I shall remain curious and examine the data as suggested by the likes of Steven Pinker and the team at RethinkX. I want to know where we're heading and at what pace. I shall follow the thought leaders who are researching what we need to do to be more connected, more peaceful, healthier, able to enjoy abundant resources and infinite opportunities and to do so with discernment and wisdom.

Over and above this, I am persuaded that (a) Wisdom will be a massive ingredient of our brighter future and (b) that conscious Purposeful Alignment is key to delivering the world that most of us want to see.

For these reasons, please join me in Parts III and IV to further explore the nature of Wisdom and how we might grow our own, and finally why Alignment is so powerful.

Notes

1 Russell Evans: www.linkedin.com/in/russellevansprimeast/
2 Gary Edwards: www.linkedin.com/in/garyedwardsprimeast/

Part III

The Wisdom Code

Why mankind needs a new approach to personal, corporate and global leadership

Why wisdom and why now? 10

As already explained in this book, especially in Chapter 6, the need for Wisdom was a thread that came up time and time again in the workshops I ran for audiences from schools, further education, professional institutions and businesses. These were audiences of all ages from seven to well over seventy, from school children to retirees. In the brighter future that people envisaged, wise leadership across every sector of society was mentioned time and time again.

In particular, people wanted to see leaders who cared more about creating a brighter future for generations to come than short-termism or mere financial success. It made me realise that "wise leadership" now, more than ever, needs to be a priority and an oft-used term going forward.

This need takes account of the disruption we have already spoken of: the challenges of a climate crisis; a global pandemic; multiple wars between nations; failing economies; as well as unprecedented, interlinked and simultaneous disruption across sectors of industry such as energy, transport, food, labour, manufacturing and information. These industrial disruptions have the capacity to mitigate all the adverse challenges we face, but only if they are grasped wisely and in empathetic collaboration with all affected parties. If that doesn't make the case for wisdom, I don't know what does.

At headline level, I describe Wisdom as doing the right thing in the right way at the right time. How does this compare with a more comprehensive definition? The Oxford English Dictionary has this to say:[1]

DOI: 10.4324/9781003428121-14

162 The Wisdom Code

Wisdom: Capacity of judging rightly in matters relating to life and conduct; soundness of judgement in the choice of means and ends; sometimes, less strictly, sound sense, esp. in practical affairs: opposed to folly.

ACTIVITY: WISE LEADERSHIP WITH JACK KORNFIELD

You can find Jack Kornfield's dharma talk given on Presidents Day, 2016, at Spirit Rock Meditation Centre.[2] Listen as Kornfield shares the qualities of leadership taught by the Buddha: generosity, integrity, non-harming, steadiness, sacrifice, patience, inclusiveness, vision, trust and loving awareness.

Note what Kornfield has to say about the respective wisdom from Presidents Washington and Lincoln and how he uses the event of President's Day to get his message across. Make notes in your journal on your key learning and what inspired you most about his talk.

I especially liked how he shared the perspective of the Buddha during the time he spent with leaders. I made the following notes, somewhat paraphrased:

If a nation or a society comes together in harmony, listens to one another in harmony and departs in harmony, if they treat all the members of the society with respect, if they protect those who are vulnerable, children, women, those who are older, those who are sick; if they tend to the teachings of their ancestors and elders that carry wisdom and if they tend to the natural environment around them then they can be expected to prosper and not decline.

I noted that Leadership in times of change, wise leadership, starts with generosity, integrity, non-harming, steadiness, sacrifice, consideration of the whole, flexibility, patience, inclusivity, vision and trust. Also, these things can be trained.

Furthermore, Kornfield talks about the innate connection between the wisdom of human beings (which we assume comes with experience) and the innate wisdom of children – empathy, love and compassion.

Notice how he makes the point that we really are connected in consciousness (and in breath) and that being present requires us to listen deeply with an open heart and from that place to respond with loving awareness and mindfulness.

Note what he says about the different kinds of love – I hope this resonates with much of what I proposed in Chapter 1.

What did you think about Kornfield's perspective on Compassion and how to act with a "noble" heart of love? How did this play out in his account of the Wisdom of President Jimmy Carter in meeting President Nixon at the White House?

I trust that this meditation on Wisdom in leadership will transform your heart and make the case for growing Wisdom with practice. Just imagine how our world would be transformed if the world's leaders spoke with each other in love, encouraging us to live in the "immediacy of our life and in eternity" – what a powerful thought.

The question is not the future of humanity but the presence of eternity

In Part II, we acknowledged the different characters at play in the challenges we face. We affirmed the tendency for many of us to think and operate in silos. We looked at the risks associated with failure to engage and listen.

You will be more than aware by now that Wisdom was my sixth aspiration for a brighter future. It is an aspiration to which no particular Sustainable Development Goal (SDG) was attributed during my analysis. Yet it is an aspiration, it could be argued, that runs as a thread through all 17 goals.

Is the world awakening to the need for Wisdom?

In 2015, I aligned my focus on Purposeful Leadership to the United Nations' 17 SDGs – this being the greatest purpose we could achieve. Or, as I put it in the subtitle of my book *Designing the Purposeful World*, "a blueprint for humanity".

Since 2015, I've noticed a movement for leaders to do what is often regarded as "inner work" as a prerequisite to delivering on global imperatives. Perhaps the most widely known initiative in this respect is the "Inner Development Goals" or IDGs (very easy to find online).

The IDGs were officially founded in 2020 by Ekskäret Foundation,[3] the New Division and 29k Foundation together with a group of researchers, experts and practitioners in leadership development and sustainability.

164 The Wisdom Code

The IDGs aim to simplify and make accessible the knowledge already existing in the field. The basis of this work is grounded in a science-based understanding of inner development and, particularly, what is needed to support a sustainable future. This enquiry is about synthesising a complex field of inner development into a framework that helps to name, understand and communicate the change that's needed.

The IDGs are supported by various thought-leaders as Senior Scientific Advisors. They are well-respected subject-matter experts who have been prolific in the field of adult development. They include

- Amy C. Edmondson, Ph.D., Harvard Business School
- Jennifer Garvey Berger, Ph.D., Harvard University
- Robert Kegan, Ph.D., Harvard University
- Renée Lertzman, Ph.D., Cardiff University
- Otto Scharmer, Senior Lecturer, MIT Sloan School of Management
- Peter Senge, Senior Lecturer, MIT Sloan School of Management
- Daniel J. Siegel, MD UCLA

In a way, the advent of the IDGs, five years after the SDGs, is a product of the very same logic that gave rise to the sixth aspiration in this book. The only difference is naming it "Wisdom" simply because I truly believe that's what the world wants – and making it one of six aspirations as a visible inclusion – just as vital as the other five.

Wisdom – the golden thread

Nevertheless, if wisdom is a thread that runs through the SDGs, by inference it must be a thread that similarly runs through the five other aspirations. Let's put that to the test.

Wisdom in connection

As a reminder, our first aspiration encompasses a vast range of ways that humans connect with each other – physically, digitally, socially and emotionally. Connection (in all its forms) takes time and energy and, if we want to live a life that maximises our impact on a brighter future, we must manage all aspects of connection with great skill and wisdom. In the digital world, connection has never been easier. We have access to an infinite amount of information and perspectives. We could easily be seduced into consuming lots of content, most of which would be assembled by algorithms to pander to our taste and prejudices. We could equally be drawn into polarised and angry debates with those of opposite views who have no intention to participate in constructive and fruitful conversation. Thus, we need to ration our use of digital systems and allocate our time with discernment. The same applies to our use of communication mechanisms, whether email, messaging or physical or virtual meetings. It is so easy to be consumed by the machine.

Exactly the same logic applies to other forms of connection. Who do we spend time with and for what reason? Conversely, who needs our time, attention, expertise, love and compassion?

ACTIVITY

Make a list of the people you spend most time with and your reasons for doing so.

Add in any others who it is important to spend time with. Add a couple of columns against each name or class of person to record the time you spend with them and perhaps a "marks out of ten" rating for the importance of your relationship with them.

Review your notes and make a note of any changes you could wisely make to your allocation of time.

The above exercise is particularly important when we have so many options on how to meet with people. One example is the work I do as a leadership coach. Until recently, most of my coaching was done face-to-face. However, during the recent global pandemic, all my coaching took place online. Professional people have got used to working this way. However, more and more they are also valuing contact in person. For most of my clients, depending on geography, we try and meet in person once out of every three occasions.

Navigating the more emotional aspects of connection requires just as much, if not more wisdom. Friends and family, for most of us, can be particularly difficult to manage in a satisfactory manner. Even within families, people have different needs which may vary over time. It's not just how often we see them, it's also what we do with time together and how we engage with them. We should include those close to us in the audit we

166 The Wisdom Code

conducted in the last activity above and contemplate what we might need to do differently.

I realise that these thoughts on wisdom in connection are really only the tip of a huge iceberg. We will always have scope to improve the way we connect. Wisdom suggests we spend time contemplating such matters and seek to improve over time. I hope you find the Wisdom Code diagnostic later in this book to be helpful in raising your awareness to tuning your approach.

Wisdom in peacemaking

At first thought, in all probability, few of us would consider ourselves to be peacemakers. Similarly, whilst we would probably all like to see world peace in our lifetimes, we may feel completely helpless in making it so. That was definitely the way I felt about peace before writing this book. Now I realise the plethora of ways that I can and do contribute to a more peaceful world.

Here are my top ten in order of the impact I suspect they make

1. Including peace as one of just six aspirations for a brighter future in this book and the associated events I get to speak at or facilitate.
2. Culture-change programmes where I help clients to measure the culture they have (including associated entropy and conflict) as well as the culture they need to deliver their purpose and vision (almost always a more harmonious way of working).
3. Coaching leaders in purposeful leadership which frequently involves dealing with challenging situations and potential conflicts and where leading with creativity and positive intelligence is a more productive and harmonious approach.
4. As a father, family member and friend, listening with empathy to the challenges of those I love and helping them as best as I'm able to navigate challenges and conflicts wisely.
5. Acting as a mediator in any conflict situations where I have the opportunity to be helpful.
6. Using my democratic vote to support politicians who show a wise approach to peace building, including the establishment of Departments for Peace.

7. Being kind and courteous as I go about my life – with everyone I meet, especially where there is inherent scope for conflict such as on roads or in public transport.
8. Refraining from judgement of people or situations and taking the time to be positive and creative rather than reactive.
9. Taking time to apologise and make it up to people where I have caused distress of any kind.
10. Encouraging anyone I meet who is making the world a more peaceful place.

ACTIVITY: HOW ABOUT YOU?

Make your own list in your journal of the top ten ways you are making the world a more peaceful place. How could you leverage your approach to make it even more impactful?

There is so much wisdom in any act of peacemaking. Families and friendships are happier and more productive; organisations are harmonious and productive; communities thrive; and the ultimate is that we injure or kill fewer people and make it easier to make the world a better place.

Wisdom in vitality

Wisdom is very much about having a broad long-term world view. It is about doing the right thing in the right way at the right time. When it comes to vitality and the well-being of ourselves, other people, humanity and the world we live in, we have sadly fallen into unwise habits that deliver short-term gains at the expense of longer-term benefits. This applies to all walks of life. We work long hours to acquire material goods and thereby limit our lives and happiness. We fail to invest in the well-being of our workforces and wonder why people leave to work elsewhere. And we show disrespect to the world we live in, undervaluing ecosystems and the climate we depend on for our survival.

Sadly, most of us fall into these traps. I know that I do. Every year I map a set of goals against each of my personal values. For the last ten years, the goals I have been most prone to failing are the ones mapped against Vitality.

168 The Wisdom Code

I'm ashamed to admit that I tend to wait for my health to decline before I do something about it.

I rather suspect the same applies at a global scale. For example, in the case of perhaps our biggest challenge, the climate, my suspicion is that the human race will succeed in doing the right thing, right at the last minute. We have the means to tackle the climate challenge, but I suspect we will suffer far too many avoidable adverse weather conditions, fires, floods, loss of habitat, rises in sea levels, forced migration of populations and all the associated conflicts before we start to see an inevitable light at the end of the tunnel, and the delivery of a predictable brighter future for us all.

Wisdom in abundance

I have been convinced by the innovators, entrepreneurs and specialists that we have the wherewithal to secure sufficient resources, energy, food, money and services for the whole human race to live happy and joyful lives in harmony with other life forms on our precious world. However, the word sufficient is key. I mean sufficient for everyone's need, and not their greed. And this doesn't mean living as paupers on the verge of poverty. Technology is advancing so fast that the quality of our lives will be astounding within as little as a decade or two, provided we advance with a sense of wisdom and alignment. Cheap, abundant energy, transport, food, labour and intelligence alone have the potential for this transformation. Just about every other condition for our brighter future is enabled by these advances.

Notice my use of the word "alignment" in the previous paragraph. We have the opportunity to use the benefits from progress in our first aspiration (connection) to consciously align the whole of society to the same vision. This is the power of the concepts proposed in this book. Imagine a world where collaboration is preferred to competition, where encouragement is more prevalent than sabotage, where innovation is shared in a spirit of mutual gain. Look for example how quickly the world worked together to develop vaccines to tackle the Covid-19 pandemic. Despite some notable failures to respond with wisdom and to protect some of our most vulnerable people and populations, this was nevertheless an impressive achievement. We will return to this essential topic of alignment in the last section and concluding chapter of this book.

Wisdom in opportunity

The technological advances described above and throughout this book can and should present massive opportunities for everyone, indeed for all of life on our planet. Whilst many will see such advances as a threat to livelihoods (which they are), for every job that is replaced by technology, there will be many more opportunities created, but only if we manage the transition with a high degree of wisdom. We absolutely must adopt a strategic approach to leverage change "for the many, not the few". We need to support people to achieve financial security by considering alternative economic systems such as Universal Basic Income funded by more efficient industries and a significant increase in the trade of carbon credits to facilitate carbon sequestration. We need to seize educational advances for all of society at any age throughout our global society.

To what extent do we dare to dream?

As one tiny example close to my heart, I can easily imagine a time when some form of artificial intelligence will seamlessly conduct an audit of who we are, all our successes, achievements, qualifications, skills, strengths, preferences, lifestyle needs, interests, values and beliefs and will present the most interesting, inspiring and valuable learning to us, with a calculated view to enabling us to lead our happiest, most fulfilling life and one that delivers powerful benefits to the world in conscious alignment to our brighter future.

Chapter summary

If Wisdom really is the golden thread that binds our aspirations for a brighter future together, then it makes sense that each one of us takes time to consciously strengthen our Wisdom muscles.

In the next chapter, I offer something I refer to as the "Wisdom Code". I researched this method by reading extensively about the subject of Wisdom, contemplating what makes us Wise and suggesting a set of exercises that we can choose from in order to inform our personal development plan.

I stress that this is not intended to be a comprehensive "all you need to know about Wisdom" go-to. Nor is it essential in all its component parts.

170 The Wisdom Code

Rather, it is intended to be a stimulus for action, further contemplation, new insights and even more action of your own design.

I hope you enjoy the journey.

Notes

1 Oxford University Press, 2024. *Oxford English Dictionary* – "Wisdom": www. oed.com/dictionary/wisdom_n?tab=pronunciation&tl=true
2 Spirit Rock Meditation Center, 2016. Jack Kornfield's dharma talk given on Presidents Day, 2016, at Spirit Rock Meditation Centre: https://youtu.be/ M19G5DjUSzc?si=hzORyPEOKDSAOcLB
3 Inner Development Goals, 2024. www.innerdevelopmentgoals.org/about

The Wisdom Code   11

I deliberately made Wisdom the sixth aspiration, something of vital importance to focus on into the future, something we especially need to focus on right now.

Let me be absolutely clear. There are many ways to develop wisdom. It was hinted at above by Jack Kornfield. There are plenty of valuable exercises associated with the Inner Development Goals and the stages of adult development. I strongly encourage you to explore.

This chapter explores and provides examples of 18 sources of modern-day wisdom, allocated to just three categories. I have derived them from my own research and personal experience.

Just as in the first two parts of this book, my aim is not to be prescriptive, but rather to suggest a curriculum comprising a few practical ways we can all develop wisdom, as individuals and as organisations. Doubtless there will be other ways, and I encourage you to add and explore your own topics and exercises according to your needs and preferences.

The three categories, each with their six sources of wisdom are as follows:

Attitude (self-awareness)

- Simplicity
- Prudence
- Gratitude
- Presence

DOI: 10.4324/9781003428121-15

172 The Wisdom Code

- Curiosity
- Authenticity

Action

- Exploration
- Experience
- Learning
- Contemplation
- Foresight
- Service

Relationship

- Collaboration
- Listening
- Empathy
- Open-mindedness
- Kindness
- Non-judgement

Outcomes

The idea is that, as we practice each source of wisdom, we will act with discernment and, as suggested earlier in this book, we will hence be more likely to "do the right thing, in the right way at the right time".

The consequential outcome, I suggest, will indeed be a wiser and brighter future as defined by our six aspirations.

Time to take stock on some wisdom options

Below is a simple stock-take that enables us to check how well we are living the "Wisdom Code". For each of the 18 sources of wisdom listed above, there are six statements describing how they might play out in our lives. So, in all, we have 108 opportunities to reflect and improve. For each opportunity, in the margin or your journal, score the extent it is playing out where

The Wisdom Code **173**

0 is "not at all" and 10 is "totally". Also, score the extent you would like it to be in a year's time and what simple new habit or action would make it so.

Alternatively, if you'd like a swifter way to engage with this thinking, simply take a highlighter or pencil and mark the items that resonate, providing clues for your later attention.

Simplicity

- I have just the right amount of complexity in my life to support my personal purpose
- I have given away possessions that no longer serve a useful purpose
- My routine is focused on people and pursuits I really value with space in between to deal with the unexpected and stay calm
- I enjoy the simple things in life and sharing them with others
- I have simplified tasks and processes that I use in my life and work
- The simplicity of my life leaves me time for reflection, contemplation and kindness

Prudence

- I take care of things I own or have access to
- I don't create waste
- I live well within my means and I'm not extravagant
- I take time to understand my circumstances
- I plan for success and expect the unexpected
- I am rational in my decisions

Gratitude

- I am grateful for my life and the opportunities it provides
- I am grateful for the encouragement of others to be the best I can be
- I appreciate others and show my appreciation in ways that will encourage them
- I am grateful for our world, the complexity of life and how amazing things just seem to work
- I am grateful for family and friends
- I reflect each day and take stock of my gratitude

174   The Wisdom Code

Presence

- I live in the moment
- I deal with problems that are past or future-focused and then put them aside to focus on now
- When I'm with others, I listen attentively and respect their view whether I agree or not
- I make eye (or other respectful) contact to truly see those I am with
- I try to remember to use people's preferred names
- I respect and do not judge others

Curiosity

- I have a healthy curiosity in people and matters I care about
- If I don't know something about a subject that's important to me, I will research it until I have learnt sufficient for now
- I am always learning
- I have a plan for learning
- When things don't go as planned, I look for learning and opportunities
- I take an interest in what other people do and offer encouragement where this is helpful

Authenticity

- I know who I am
- I can articulate my purpose and values
- I will speak up on my beliefs when it makes sense to do so
- People know who I am and what I stand for
- I know my strengths and play to them as much as possible
- I make a conscious effort to share my expertise for the benefit of others

Exploration

- I enjoy visiting and experiencing new places
- My travels and adventures help me to see new perspectives

The Wisdom Code **175**

- I like meeting new people and learning their stories
- My life is a great adventure that I treasure
- I treat learning as an exploration
- I enjoy exploring and discovering who I really am

Experience

- I value the experiences I have had that make me who I am
- I consciously create and pursue new experiences
- I do not allow fear of failure to stop me learning from life
- My life is a rich tapestry of experiences that I treasure
- I take the opportunity to visit people and places that stimulate my personal development
- I proactively create and share inspirational experiences with others

Learning

- I am grateful for all the teachers I have had in my life – formal and informal
- I have made many mistakes and learnt from most of them
- I keep a record of my learning – this encourages me to learn even more
- I am in control of my lifelong learning and have short- and long-term plans that are "in play"
- I encourage others to learn
- I am consciously developing my personal strengths in order to be of service to the world

Contemplation

- I spend time alone thinking about the meaning of life
- I meditate and I spend time in nature
- I reflect on things that have happened and make sense of them
- I take time to consider my options in life
- I make plans for the future and take life as it comes
- I spend time with special others to discuss things that matter to us

176 The Wisdom Code

Foresight

- I take notice of things that are happening in the world
- I notice trends in life
- I anticipate opportunities and risks and I plan accordingly
- I have a vision for a brighter future
- I have a sense of personal calling
- I am curious to explore the predictions of specialists

Service

- I serve causes and people that matter to me
- My work is aligned with my personal values
- My work is helping to make the world a better place
- I am in the driver's seat of my own career
- I strive to bring my best self into the service of others
- I have a strong sense of purpose

Collaboration

- I spend time with others who share my interests
- I am happy to compare notes with others who don't share my views
- I have a strong support network of people I trust and can confide in
- I enjoy learning with and from other people
- If I need to know something, I'm very happy to ask someone
- If I think I can help others, I will actively share what I know or offer a practical hand

Listening

- When I listen, I do so with full attention
- I listen with an open mind, not just to reinforce my opinion
- I listen with an open heart, noticing and taking account of other's feelings
- As I listen to others, I am conscious and supportive of the prospect of a brighter future

The Wisdom Code   **177**

- I make space for others to be heard, especially those who find it hard to be heard
- I listen to learn and understand, not simply to respond

Empathy

- As I notice things happening to others, I allow myself to sense their feelings
- I feel the pain and joy of other people
- I sense the emotions of others
- I care deeply for other people and all of life in our world
- I feel connected to the ecosystem we call life
- I give space and encouragement for people to express fully how they feel

Open-mindedness

- I am open to new learning
- I am happy to hear from people who are different from me
- I realise that I don't know all the answers
- I am happy to be proved wrong
- There are so many people who know better than I do
- I look for learning from people who have contra opinions to me

Kindness

- I make time in my day to be kind to others
- If I'm able to help someone in need I do
- When I have to choose a response, kindness plays a significant part
- I look for, notice and take opportunities to be kind
- Kindness matters more to me than getting my own way
- My kindness is not dependent on my opinion of a person

Non-judgement

- I do not judge other people
- I do not judge myself for my past actions but I do learn from them

178 The Wisdom Code

- I respect the values and choices of other people
- I am happy to be with others, even if we think differently
- I prefer freedom and empowerment to control and manipulation
- I am kind to myself and others as we learn and grow together

ACTIVITY

Once you've considered each statement, marked the extent to which you live it and the extent you'd like to live it, pick a small number of the statements to work on. What action could you take to begin to train your wisdom muscles?

Part IV

Global alignment

Total and conscious alignment to a brighter future

12

Somewhere in time

> A spark
> A simple burst of light
> Unseen
> Unseen by many
> By all
> But one
>
> And not for the first time
> For the first was seen
> But unnoticed
> As was the second
> And the third
>
> But this time
> Was the right time
> And right space
> And right mind
> The right context
>
> The spark has landed
> On dry tinder
> And the breeze is just right
> Gentle

182 Global alignment

Not too strong
Persistent and enduring
Breathing life

In a moment a flame
Reaching out
Catching substance
Consuming and creating
Warmth
Light
Fascination
Inspiration

A tiny flame
A little attention
More fuel
And more fuel
An inferno

Energy capable of awesome wonder
Powerful
Not just of action
But of reaction
And chain reaction
Perpetual
From a spark[1]

Thank you for joining me on this exciting journey to the prospect of a brighter future for all humanity and for this fabulous world we call home. I trust that, by now, you will have reached the same or at least a similar conclusion as me. My conclusion is that a brighter future is on its way unless we are unwise and really mess things up, which I'm trusting will not be the case. The question is not "If?" but "When and how?" And the answers to these questions are up to us.

Earlier in this book, I suggested that my belief is that we will achieve this future, and my educated guess (for that is what it is) is that significant progress will be made in the next 20 years and total delivery will occur this century, heralding a new dawn for the twenty-second century. I see it playing out rather in accordance with Pareto's principle. That is to say that, in a given period, 80% of the gain will be made in 20% of the time it will take for complete delivery. Of course, delivering on the expectations we have for a brighter future today does not mean progress will cease thereafter. Far from it.

When we are living wise, healthy, loving, compassionate and connected lives in peace on this planet, when we have secured abundance for all people and the opportunity for us all to live our most meaningful lives, we will do what humanity has always done. We will ask the question, "What next?" In fact, there will be nine billion of us, all asking similar questions, sharing ideas and encouraging each other. Our interconnectivity will also mean that these ideas will be shared with those most suited to hear them, thanks to the intelligence built into our future systems.

By this time, we will, in all probability, have ventured further into space. We may well have begun to establish communities on other planets. We will be making sense of what it means to be an interplanetary species, thus extending the survival of humanity beyond the life of our planet. At the same time, we may be proficient in extending the life of our planet by being able to facilitate ideal climate, ecosystems and other conditions. We will also have the time and the wherewithal, thanks to the labour-saving potential of artificial intelligence, to anticipate and guard against potentially catastrophic events.

My suspicion and lived experience is that the speed with which we deliver our brighter future will depend on the global alignment of leadership. That is why this book is titled *Leading Beyond Sustainability*. In my previous books, *Designing the Purposeful Organization* (Kogan Page 2015) and *Designing the Purposeful World* (Routledge 2018), I emphasised how much leadership has evolved in the last 50 years or so. Instead of "leaders making things happen" which is a version of the mantra of a bygone age, I proposed that "leaders see a better future and consciously create the conditions in which it will happen". In this book, only one word of that more progressive mantra has changed. I have replaced "better" with "brighter". Perhaps it reflects the concept of a bright light at the end of a somewhat darker tunnel, or the thought of the sun rising on a new age, and I do confess to being inspired by Adam Dorr's powerful book *Brighter: Optimism, Progress, and the Future of Environmentalism*. I now define "Purposeful Leadership" as:

consciously creating the conditions for a brighter future

As I reach this point in writing this book, I realise that I do so with a strong sense of understanding of how my work in Purposeful Leadership has been

184 Global alignment

a journey from one place to another. It started with a need to understand how corporate culture fitted into corporate strategy. I realised that the focal point for all strategies was "purpose". That led to my thinking about "purposeful organisations" and from there to the concept of a "purposeful word" (stimulated by the United Nations Sustainable Development Goals (SDGs)) and from there to the shared purpose and positivity of a brighter future.

It is only by each of us contemplating our journey that we get to make sense of it. All this reminds me of a poem I wrote for my daughter Jenny in 2019 and which I'd like to share with you now. I hope it inspires you to contemplate your own journey "from somewhere to somewhere else".

Somewhere

> Somewhere
> Somewhere in the world is a place
> That is drawing me closer
> I know not the place
> I just know which way I face
> I feel not perplexed
> I just know what next
>
> The world presents
> Presents so many gifts
> Of promise, of concern,
> Of challenge, a path on which to turn
>
> The gaze of a friend draws me in
> It feels like a great place to begin
> I lose myself to this new adventure
> I follow
> No care for life's other concerns
> I follow
> Simply follow
>
> In this way
> I trust the consciousness of a thousand generations
> On this day
> I let go of plans and comfortable temptations

I dare to go
With the flow
To where I cannot know

On this day
My foolish pride no longer tries
To dictate the pace
To try and win the race

What race?

On this day I abandon myself
To joy and adventure

And when
When, after many years
After many years
Of sorrow and of joy
I look back on this journey
And reconstruct the story
I will sigh
A big, big sigh
And say "My ...
I came such a long way
From somewhere
To somewhere else"

And I shall smile
A big, big smile
Knowing full well
That somewhere
Is, and always has been, home.[2]

The alignment of eight conditions for a brighter future

So, it is only fitting that we should conclude this book with a reminder of the
eight conditions that Purposeful Leaders must create and some brief words
on how they play out in the delivery of our brighter future. These eight
conditions haven't changed since I first drew the PrimeFocus framework

Global alignment

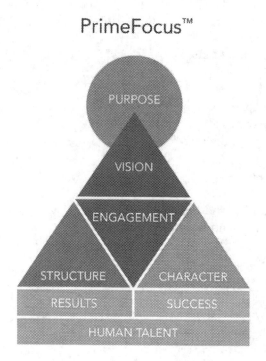

Figure 12.1 PrimeFocus™.
Source: © primeast 2008, www.primeast.com

in the 1990s to help leaders in the UK electricity industry understand the importance of culture change (Figure 12.1).

A shared purpose for our species

Our guiding north star is always "Purpose". It is the "why" of what we do. This may seem simple but, in my 20-plus years of experience in Purposeful Leadership, I have come across senior leaders who vastly undersell the purpose of their organisations. There are examples of such organisations in this book, organisations whose people thought their purpose was to "write software", "fabricate ductwork" or "educate young people".

Of course, their leaders knew all too well who their customers were and why they in turn needed the services they procured. But rarely do such organisations truly celebrate the significant impact they are having on the delivery of our brighter future. If they did, they would be able to inspire

Total and conscious alignment to a brighter future **187**

their various stakeholders to engage with them, securing loyal customers, suppliers, shareholders and employees. This has to be good for performance, sales, staff retention, morale and much more. I recommend that every organisation on the planet should contemplate our six aspirations for a brighter future and work out where and how they fit in, thereby articulating their purpose and brand in the most inspiring manner possible.

This is powerful in its own right, and that power is magnified with the conscious alignment thereto of everything the organisation or individual does. In summary, the purpose of any organisation is to play its part in the delivery of a brighter future, expressed in terms of their particular specialism and with reference to at least one of the six aspirations or some subset thereof.

I usually engage organisations on the topic of purpose and help them to see their inspiring purpose through the eyes of all stakeholders, ideally by involving as many of these groups as they feel able. For example, recently I did this with all the staff at a group of colleges in the UK. We began by considering their purpose through the eyes of staff, then through the eyes of pupils, then through the eyes of society. Finally, we were able to identify which of the UN SDGs they had the most impact on. We could equally have used the six aspirations had they been defined at that time.

A compelling vision

Once an organisation's purpose is known and articulated, those involved should be in a perfect position to contemplate and define a vision that will inspire all stakeholders to play their best part in the quest. Whilst Purpose explains why a journey is desirable, Vision confirms the destination.

I often get involved in facilitating senior leadership teams in this "co-creation" of the future. I usually begin by discussing all that's happening in the world, including disruption (adverse and positive). I take time to emphasise the pace of change and will ask, "How far ahead do you dare look?" and "What is your most valuable time horizon?" Once we've immersed ourselves in this time horizon and got a sense of what the world will be like, we can then co-create the vision for the organisation, either using polling software or the old-fashioned way with sticky notes on a wall. If the exercise is done well, those involved are usually surprised at the synergy between their perspectives and how easy it is to define the shared vision for their organisation.

188 Global alignment

Purposeful engagement

The above group work for creating a vision is indeed one form of Purposeful Engagement. However, when our global societal perspective is considered, it becomes clear that we will need to engage with many parties, from staff, through leadership teams, shareholders, customers, supply chains, industry groups, the communities we impact and so on. We are not the only ones on this journey, and the more people we can take with us, the better.

It is good to take time to take stock of our stakeholders and establish a stakeholder plan, identifying who we need to engage with, how often, where and on what issues.

Efficient and robust structure

Our stakeholder plan is just one of the pieces of structure that will take us to our vision. There will be many more, and there will be clues to some of the most important structures, processes and plans in our purpose and vision. With these two strategic objectives in mind, we can audit our structures and work out how they need to evolve in order to make us more efficient.

Another exercise I conduct with leadership teams is to test the vision for associated blockages, issues and opportunities. This exercise may also identify structures that need to change or behavioural issues to be dealt with. Speaking of which...

A character to deliver our brighter future

As well as considering the structures and processes that will help to deliver our purpose and vision, we also need to consider the "character" of our operation. This is a complex weave of beliefs, values and behaviours that make up our culture. I use the word "character" simply because it's equally transferrable to speak of the beliefs, values and behaviours of any individual (where we wouldn't use the word "culture" as a descriptor). This is especially useful when we try and tune our personal leadership to an agreed corporate vision.

Once an organisation has made the connection to the part it will play in delivering a brighter future, there is every chance that the culture will need to evolve to support maximum progress to the new purpose and vision.

For example, the values required by an organisation that is trying to play its maximum part in changing the world may well be very different from one that is delivering a steady-state operation (if there is such a thing these days). The bigger the goal, the more progressive and dynamic the culture may need to be.

Organisations involved in such a transition should certainly make sure they have professional support in the measurement and management of values and culture in order to diagnose the change in a systematic and well-researched manner – as opposed to simply relying on gutfeel. We said more about this earlier when I celebrated the work of many respected culture change professionals such as Richard Barrett, Owen Wibberley, Jesse Rowell, Phil Clothier, Torr Eneroth and the team at Primeast.

Results

It makes sense to measure our progress towards our new vision. We probably need to review our organisation's key performance indicators or KPIs so we can tell how quickly we're progressing. This isn't simply to correct slow performance. In an age where we're playing our part in delivering a brighter future, if we find we can move quicker than expected, we probably should capitalise on this and share the associated insights with the world so that a global joined-up approach can be achieved.

Success

In my previous published books, I have suggested that Success differs from Results. The latter are left-brain measurements to track our progress to the vision. Hence, they are shown to the left of PrimeFocus. Success, on the other hand, is very much a felt sense of achievement that likely varies from person to person, even if they're involved in the same endeavours. I always encourage organisations to get people together to share what success means to them. This is best done once the most inspiring purpose has been defined. For example, for Poppleton, mentioned in Chapter 2, the company could celebrate the installation of ductwork in a building. However, knowing that the ducts have been installed (for example) in a children's hospital for cancer treatment informs a more meaningful celebration of success.

Talent

Finally, we come to the eighth condition in PrimeFocus. If we are going to make our maximum impact on delivering our brighter future, we need to make sure we have the people (or AI) skills to do so. This will be massively impacted by the rate of change and our vision. We must start with the end in mind. If our vision is long term, we probably won't even know all the talents we will need amongst our workforce. That shouldn't stop us from having a plan.

In *Designing the Purposeful Organisation* I introduced an eight-step framework to support the development of a progressive Talent Management strategy:

1. **DIRECTION** – acknowledge the purpose and vision of the organisation and affirm that the talent strategy is there to support delivery.
2. **PHILOSOPHY** – what the organisation believes about talent really matters. There's a big difference between thinking that we only need competence of all our people and really believing in nurturing strengths. There's also a big difference between focusing on the top 10% or 20% of our people (the so-called "high-potentials") and maximising the talents of all our people. For most of the organisations I have worked with, they have adopted some variation on the following philosophy: "we will recognise, value, develop and use the unique strengths of all our people in the delivery of our purpose and vision".
3. **PROCESS** – with the direction and philosophy in mind, we can audit our whole talent management pipeline from securing talent from society, through recruitment, development, performance management, well-being, career management and so on – right through to helping them move on after their work or career has come to an end.
4. **PLAN** – the audit of our talent management systems and processes will inform what might need to change in order to tune it to our purpose and vision. This should be confirmed in a talent management plan.
5. **COMMUNICATE** – once a plan is formed, we should communicate it with all parties that need to know. This can be used to kick-off the involvement of leaders and teams as shown in steps 6 and 7.
6. **LEADERSHIP** – a progressive talent management strategy requires a certain style of leadership. This is a culture where people right down to the "factory floor" own their own talents, strengths, development plans, career plans, performance plans and so on. You will recall how one of the organisations in my personal encounters talked about

putting its people "in the driver's seat of their careers". This part of the strategy will explain how leaders will be equipped to facilitate such an evolution, including the identification of their own personal strengths, understanding how they add value, how they can be developed and put to the best use. Note this is a playing out of the "Philosophy" described in step 2 above.

7. **TEAMWORK** – a natural progression from developing leaders so they can facilitate the talent management strategy is to involve them in the development of high-performing teams. These are teams that truly understand the difference they are making in the world and how best to play to the various strengths of team members in a joined-up way.

8. **REVIEW** – finally, all good change management processes should incorporate review – as frequently as is necessary to make sure the system works and evolves as the organisation nears its vision.

I hope you find this eight-step process and the PrimeFocus framework useful. There is much more detail in *Designing the Purposeful Organization* should you need it.

The main point to make here is how the Purpose and its associated conditions (PrimeFocus) for an organisation relate upwards to the purpose (a brighter future) for humanity and the associated vision (the six aspirations). It is no different to the way the purpose of an individual should be a subset of the purpose of the team they are part of, which in turn is a subset of the same for the organisation.

Informed action

So, we come to "crunch time". I wrote this book to inspire aligned leadership throughout society to the brighter future we all seek. This brighter future, comprising its six aspirations, is not something I dreamed up. Rather it is something I have heard thousands of people describe time and time again in workshops and discussions, ever since world leaders signed on to the UN SDGs in New York in September 2015. This engagement was my way of raising awareness of the SDGs and accelerating their delivery in the only way I knew how.

In a way, the timing of this book is prompted by the realisation that millions of people are already working towards the delivery of a brighter future. Also, those who seem to have the greatest success are those who are working with the natural ecological, technological and economic

192 Global alignment

forces that are there to facilitate our understanding. They are led by wise leaders who know how to accelerate progress through the telling of compelling narratives and action focused on the global good and the longer-term needs of humanity and our world. They use the power of reason and vision to take people with them, to prompt our further curiosity and collaboration.

I emphasise a sentiment I expressed earlier, in not so many words, that the exact description of the six aspirations is not what's important. Rather it's being able, as leaders (which we all are), to describe this purpose and vision in the most compelling way, suited to our respective audiences. Then to use this "north star" to align action, as described by the eight conditions in PrimeFocus. In doing so, we must bear in mind the observations clarified in Part II that we are all different and that our diversity of views and talent should never be an obstacle to collaboration and delivery. Rather, it is our diversity that has the power to fuel creativity and innovation. We must set about evolving our shared future by being, not just willing but eager, to engage and learn from people who are not like us and who we may be otherwise tempted to avoid.

Ten steps to a brighter future

I'd like to leave you with ten questions, some closed (which serve as gates to subsequent questions) and many open to give you scope to define your personal or corporate contribution:

1. Do you believe a brighter future is something we, as a species, can realistically aspire to?
2. Do you wish to play your most significant part in its delivery?
3. Are you happy therefore to weave this brighter future into your own personal purpose?
4. What would that look or sound like? Can you articulate it for yourself and for your work?
5. Do the six aspirations make sense to you? If not, how would you describe your vision of a brighter future? Whatever works for you and your audience is what's important.
6. Where in this brighter future can you and your organisation make the biggest impact? Articulate this as your own purpose and vision. Work with others as appropriate.

Total and conscious alignment to a brighter future **193**

7. Who do you need to connect and collaborate with in order to have maximum impact? Include those that come to mind from reading Part II of this book.
8. How can you use the tried and tested PrimeFocus framework to consciously create your brighter future? Maybe consider each of the eight conditions in turn to inform where you need to pay most attention in the coming weeks.
9. Who else needs to know about the concepts in this book and, in particular, the action you're taking since engaging with them?
10. How will you celebrate your progress in order to inspire others to join you on this journey?

A final and unexpected "personal encounter"

I had intended to locate all my "personal encounters" in Part I of this book and associate them with each of the six aspirations in turn. Then, just as this book was nearing completion, I received a call from a global law firm, undertaking pioneering work to inspire unprecedented action on sustainability by making the measurement of sustainability easy and accessible to anyone anywhere in the world.

The call was from Neill Morley, Senior Business Engagement Manager, at DLA Piper.[3] He explained that the firm had made sustainability its highest priority, affirming that the job of lawyers is to mitigate the risk of their clients and support them in wise strategic choices. He affirmed that the best possible decisions would always be those made in pursuance of a brighter future.

Neill had made the link between the work of his firm and the message he had read in an early summary of this book on social media.

To highlight the firm's strategic imperative, Neill drew my attention to the following quotation by the firm's Managing Director, Sustainability and Resilience, Jean-Pierre Douglas-Henry:

"We are witnessing what could be the biggest reallocation of capital in history. Sustainability and ESG (Environment, Social & Governance) has moved out of the CSR (Corporate Social Responsibility) function and into the C-suite".

I hope you enjoy this final "encounter" below. I have a feeling it will be followed, as is often the case, by another chapter of this journey that I wasn't expecting.

194 Global alignment

A FINAL PERSONAL ENCOUNTER – Neill Morley, Senior Business Engagement Manager, at DLA Piper: "Facilitating and measuring alignment to a brighter future"

I first met Neill at his office in Leeds in 2019. He and his colleagues were curious about the opportunities to align the work of their sizeable IT Department to the needs of their internal customers, principally lawyers providing services to corporate clients. My colleagues and I helped them explore ways of measuring the culture of this organisation using the Barrett methods discussed earlier in this book.

We were poised to run a survey for the company to commence in 2020, just as the workplace was disrupted by Covid-19 and other priorities for the business caused us to postpone the work.

Nevertheless, we continued to talk with Neill and his colleagues about a range of behavioural challenges and how to tackle them. In 2023, it became apparent that Neill had a personal goal to do all he could to accelerate the cause of sustainability to benefit humanity and also to seize the opportunity for his company to capitalise on its technical strengths in service of what he called *"demonstrable alignment"*. He had made the link between his own goals and those expressed in the summary of this book, which he had read and commented on via social media.

We arranged to meet for an exploratory conversation and concluded that *demonstrable alignment* to a brighter future would be a great asset to organisations wishing to show the world that they were taking their sustainability obligations sincerely. It could also be a huge motivator to any member of any workforce if they were able to test the impact of personal gains against company goals and, ultimately, global commitments such as (but not exclusively) the UN SDGs.

Neill's vision was that any individual, department or organisation should be able to record a current or intended action and conduct an immediate impact assessment in a matter of minutes.

Neill had this to say about the scope of the opportunity as he saw it from the outset:

I have been fortunate to work with many wonderfully enthusiastic colleagues connected with Sustainability.

We used a multitude of frameworks and assessment measures to report back to our International Energy and Climate Change Committee.

> I wondered if there was a specific product or tool that we could utilise to assess any work activity, no matter how small or large. Our internal and external consultants were not aware of anything, so I set out to produce our own. It needed to be simple, and intuitive enough for anyone to quickly produce high-level analysis, helping them to connect their work to Sustainability goals but could also be used by experts to satisfy complex regulatory requirements.
>
> I used our internal innovation methodology, which is based on Design Thinking principles, to work with technical engineers and our internal sustainability experts to develop the tool.
>
> We have used the tool to complete successful proof of concepts in areas such as Project Portfolio Management, Vendor Selection Process and Architecture Roadmaps.
>
> We are collaborating with our external partners, including Clive, to develop the tool, embed it into our own operations and hope to make a free version of it available to everyone.

As I write the concluding words of this book

I hope that, together, we have achieved the following:

- inspired you to approach the work you do with conscious alignment to a brighter future;
- that you now look beyond the immediate outcomes of your work to that point where you impact at least one of our six aspirations;
- that this will give you the confidence, courage and strength to persevere, even when the road ahead is challenging;
- that you will consequently encourage others to do the same and take credit for the impact they too are making;
- that you will be more likely to notice, encourage and celebrate anyone who is changing the world, in the full knowledge that, in so doing, you too are changing the world;
- that you will be more likely to connect with others in our common quest, including (or especially) those who are playing a different role or holding a different perspective than your own;
- that you will appreciate the immense value of wisdom, recognise it when you see or hear it and take conscious steps to enhance your own wisdom;

196 Global alignment

- that, as a progressive leader, you will consciously create the eight conditions for purposeful success as described in PrimeFocus and use the framework to work out a robust strategy for continuous improvement;
- that you will share these insights with others so that we can all accelerate our progress to a brighter future; and
- that you will keep in touch with me and others on this journey if only to share your progress and inspire us all to keep going.

This is a team effort

Writing this book has been, for me, the culmination of over 20 years of practice in the field of Purposeful Leadership, working with some amazing colleagues and clients. We have learnt a great deal and remain willing and able to support you in this journey. I encourage you to reach out in the spirit of collaboration if that might accelerate your journey and with it, our shared brighter future.

Thank you for your time and attention. And, when you've taken all you need from this book why not gift it or lend it to someone you know who is ready to engage with its message and join us in the delivery of a brighter future?

So, what's next?

I trust that there has been sufficient stimulation in this book for you to work out your plan for the future. I encourage you to write this down whilst your thinking is still fresh.

For me, I always find that the act of writing a book stimulates the road ahead. Looking back, it is easier to join the dots than it is by looking ahead.

My first book (of sorts) was probably my 1996 MSc dissertation on "Values and Behaviours in the Workplace". This cultivated an interest in culture change that unexpectedly served me well as a programme manager during the privatisation of the UK electricity industry. It also prompted my move away from the industry and into consultancy when my programme was successfully delivered.

I then had a few years of writing some mini-books with Primeast on "PrimeFocus", "Talent Liberation" and "Liberate Your Talent". These thoughts were largely consolidated into my first published book *Designing the Purposeful Organization – how to inspire business performance beyond boundaries* (Kogan Page 2015) which was basically a comprehensive explanation of the eight conditions shown in PrimeFocus (above). In the final chapter, I speculated that (through the power of fractal thinking) we could apply the principles of purposeful alignment to the whole world. These thoughts were articulated in 2014 just before I received an early draft of the UN SDGs and realised I had to write my second published book *Designing the Purposeful World, the UN Sustainable Development Goals as a Blueprint for Humanity* (Routledge 2018).

This book, *Leading Beyond Sustainability – six aspirations for a brighter future* is a natural successor. It was prompted in the full knowledge that the SDGs were approaching their target date. I wanted to paint a picture of a brighter future that is rational, hopeful, positive and with as few aspirations as possible in the hope we can all remember and identify with them. I also wanted to make it clear that this is a journey we are definitely on. However, naming it and discussing it, I believe will accelerate it and thereby minimise the pain, suffering and misery associated with our inevitable failures along the journey. Furthermore, I trust that, in the spirit of positivity, out of the tears of failure will emerge the learning and courage to seize the consequential opportunity. Even if we take two steps forward and one back, we eventually reach our destination.

So, that's a brief look at how my dots have joined to today. What of the future?

1. I trust that putting this book into the public domain will prompt some thoughts in people's minds, and especially in the world of work. I intend to take every opportunity to leverage this energy through inputs to conferences and workshops. I also know that my colleagues at Primeast will be keen to support any parties wishing to turn insights into action.
2. My colleague Russell Evans and I have had many conversations over 20 years about a concept we have often referred to as "Purpose Quest". We have both been immersed in the subject of Purposeful Leadership throughout this time. We have learnt a thing or two about the nature of Purpose and would like to document these, along with some new material. We suspect that Purpose is even more profound than we think it is and that most leaders don't invest nearly as much time and

energy into it as they could. Our suspicion is that, if they did, then the journey to our brighter future would be accelerated still further. What do you think?

3. When this is done, I know I have one more book in me that needs to be written. The working title is "The Clear White Light of Purpose". If you've ever listened to the song "Clear White Light" by the band Lindisfarne,[4] you'll have some idea of where I'm going with this. I hope you'll be able to join me "on the way".

Notes

1 Wilson, C. A. 2024. Poem "Somewhere in Time" by Author.
2 Wilson, C. A. 2019. Poem "Somewhere" by Author.
3 Linked In, 2024. Neill Morley: www.linkedin.com/in/neill-morley-cmgr-fcmi-67661043/
4 Lindisfarne, 2021. Lindisfarne: www.lindisfarne.co.uk/

Index

Abbott, Warwick 124
ABC News 62
abundance 29, 40–1, 61, 83–104, 135, 146, 168, 183
Adagio in G Minor 48
Adams, Bill 66, 125, 148
Africa 23, 93, 117, 157
AIESEC 24–6
alignment 5, 72, 151, 158, 168–9, 179–98
Amcara 25, 122
Anderson, Bob 14, 51, 125–6
Aperian 57–8
Arbib, James 64
archetype 8, 20, 133–42
artificial intelligence (AI) 15, 106, 110–11, 117
Asia 23, 117
aspirations 2–4, 11
Atkinson, Nathan 46, 96–7
Attenborough, Sir David 20–1, 69, 147
Australia 44, 47, 62
Axia Digital 16, 79–81

Bank of England 63
Barðdal, Thor 26
Barrett, Richard 125
Barrett Values Centre 24–6, 73, 119–20, 125

BBC 64–5, 69
Beatles 50
Belgium 23
Berners-Lee, Tim 15
Bevis, Neville 30–1
Bigwood, Luke 66–7
Biodiversity 66–7
Biswick, Luwayo 94–5
Boldt, Laurence 20
Botswana 56
Bradford, Airdale and Craven 75–7
Brahma Kumaris 26
Brexit 23, 54
Brighter (Dorr) 64, 91, 147, 183
Brin, Sergey 15
British Council 31, 55–6
Buddha 162
Buddhist Economics 84
Burford, Chris 51–2

Campbell, John 24–6, 32–3, 123–4
Carne, Dan 70–1
Carney, Mark 63
Carter, President Jimmy 163
Carver, Martin 124
Cave, Sarah 124
Cellist of Sarajevo (Galloway) 48
Century Tech 111
Chamine, Shirzad 143–4
Charles-Barks, Cara 72–3

200 Index

children 2, 14, 20, 30, 45–6, 71,
 95–6, 114, 120, 127, 133, 152,
 161–2, 189
Chubb, Paul 79–80
Clear White Light 50, 198
Clear White Light of Purpose
 (Wilson) 50
climate 1, 6, 21, 34, 56, 61–6, 70–1,
 74, 86, 91, 93–5, 98, 126, 145–8,
 161, 167–8, 183, 194
Clothier, Phil 8, 24–5, 120–2
Columbia 112
compassion 14, 17, 19–20, 22,
 24–30, 35, 40, 51, 73, 97, 124, 126,
 162–3, 165, 183
Confederation of British Industry
 (CBI) 32, 123
conflict 39–42, 46, 48, 53–5, 84, 97,
 119, 166–8, 198
connection 12–35, 39–40, 45, 49–51,
 53, 56–8, 64, 68–9, 81, 88, 102,
 107, 111, 114, 121, 128, 135, 155,
 162, 164, 188
Connors, Debbie 97–100
Covey, Steven 124
Covid 15, 67, 70, 72, 79–81, 108,
 126, 168, 194
Critical Care Passports 79–81
Crosby, Stills, Nash and Young 20
Cross Green Comprehensive
 School 50

Davison, Grace 95
democracy 15
Departments for Peace 39, 54
Designing the Purposeful Organization
 (Wilson) 1, 21, 27, 153, 183, 190,
 191, 197
Designing the Purposeful World
 (Wilson) 1, 22, 41, 112, 125, 153,
 163, 183, 197
discernment 133, 145–8, 158, 165,
 172
disease 6
DLA Piper 193–5
Dorr, Adam 64, 91, 147, 183
Douglas-Henry, Jean-Pierre
 193

ecological 14, 49, 67, 86, 95, 191
Ecopia 67–9
ecosystem 15, 19, 28, 61, 69–70, 177
education 1, 18, 40
Edwards, Gary 124, 153
Edwards-Hughes, Nigel 78
Emperor–The Perfect Penguin (Flood)
 69
energy 15, 18, 27, 29, 34, 40, 54,
 63–4, 66, 70, 73, 76, 83–5, 91–4,
 98–102, 106, 121, 124, 133, 140,
 145, 147, 154, 161, 164, 168, 182,
 194, 197–8
Energy Oasis 70, 92–3
Eneroth, Tor 8, 25, 120–3
Environment Bank 66–7
Ekskäret Foundation 163
Etheridge, Richard 79–81
Ethiopia 44–5
Ethiopian Positive Peace
 Ambassadors Programme 45
Ethiopian Reconciliation
 Commission 45
European Coal and Steel
 Community 23
European Economic Community
 (EEC) 23
European Federalist Movement 23
European Union 23, 40, 49, 117
Evans, Russell 124, 152–3, 197

Farragut 16, 87–91
fear 19
Fish, Jane 80
Flanagan, Edward J. 144
Flood, Sue 69
food 15, 40, 46, 61, 64, 83–4, 86,
 93–7, 100, 102, 111, 161, 168
forest 2, 14, 20, 38, 56, 60, 63, 65–6,
 68, 71, 94, 156
Forest Stewardship Council (FSC)
 56
fractal mathematics 5
France 23, 49

Galloway, Steven 48
Gandhi, Mahatma 49
Gaza 39

Index **201**

gender equality 34
Germany 23
Gísladóttir, Ingibjörg Sólrún 26
Global Change Data Lab 7
Global Peace Index (GPI) 42–3, 47
Global Terrorism Index 47
Globesmart 57
Gnarr, Jón 26
God 18
Good Energy 66
Google 15
government 12, 15, 21–2, 24–5, 39,
    44–5, 54, 67, 94–5, 107, 111, 139
Guardian Newspaper 63
Gura, Leo 117
Guterres, Antonio 22

habitat 1, 56, 66–7, 70–1, 86, 168
Habitat Bank 66–7
Halton Methodist Youth Club 50
Hamilton, Fergus 110
Harrogate 31, 52
Harvard University 6
Haurant, Sandra 63
Heaps, Emma 124
Hendrix, Jimi 17
Homeloan Management Limited
    (HML) 106
Hopkinson, Tim 77–9
horseshoe nail 17
Horvath, Christophe 55
*How climate change is shaping the way
    Gen Z works* (Ro) 64
How Not to Go to War 39, 54, 57
Human Synergistics 125
hunger 1, 6, 91, 95–6

Iceland 22, 26
Imperial College Health Care Trust
    80
India 49
injustice 1
Inner Development Goals (IDGs)
    163–4, 171
Institute for Economics and Peace
    (IEP) 42–4, 47–8
Israel 39
Italy 23

Jackson, Heath 67–9
Jain, Sucheta & Shail 87–91
Jessel, Marc 55–6
Jews 39
John, Wilson 30–1
journal 8, 15, 38, 41, 44, 61, 65, 66,
    99, 119, 141, 147, 149–50, 152,
    162, 167, 172
justice 34

Kakuba Literacy Project 45
Kakuba, Jude 45
karate 1
Kaye, Mike 92–3
Keller, Dr Alfred Z. 77
Killelea, Steve 42
kindness 19–20, 24, 35
King Charles 23
King Henry 16
King Richard III 16
Kornfield, Jack 162–3, 171
KPMG 67–8
Kumar, Satish 49
Kusamala 94

Lafferty, Dr Clayton 125
Leadership Circle 66, 125, 148
Leading a Purposeful Life (Wilson) 18
learning log 8
Leeds City Council 96
Lennon, John 39, 50
light trees 67–9
Lindisfarne 50
LinkedIn 8, 12, 33–4
Lipton, Bruce 4
love 13–14, 17–20, 24–30, 35, 39,
    44–5, 49–50, 52, 64, 71, 76, 88, 96,
    103, 113–14, 117, 120–1, 127, 144,
    162–3, 165–6, 198
Luxembourg 23

Maastricht Treaty 23
Malawi 30–1, 55–6, 94–5
Mandelbrot, Benoit 5
Matavai Cultural Arts Centre
    Positive Peace Workshop 47
Mauritius 56
meditation 38

Mehta, Vijay 39, 53–5, 57
Middle East 22, 40
Millennium Development Goals
    (MDGs) 21
Morgan, Sarah 124
Morley, Neill 193–5
Mozambique 56
Multicultural NSW 47
Musk, Elon 63, 93, 146

National Health Service (NHS) 16,
    72–6
NATO 40
Net Positive (Polman & Winston) 63
net zero 67
Netherlands 23
New Division 163
Nick and Linda 28–9, 155
Nixon, President 163
No Destination (Kumar) 49

oceans 2, 14, 63–8, 100, 135, 145
Olsen, Sigrún 26
Oman 26
Open Arms Infant Homes Malawi
    30–1, 94
opportunity 4, 24, 27, 29, 39–41, 45,
    58, 63, 66, 74, 84–5, 88, 98–9,
    105–15, 128, 135, 139–40, 145,
    154, 166, 168–9, 172, 175, 183,
    194, 197
optimism 6, 42, 146–7, 183
Our World in Data 6–7, 15, 39,
    41–2, 61, 85, 106, 119

Page, Larry 15
Palestine 39
pandemic 15, 54, 67, 70, 74, 79–80,
    108–9, 120, 122, 153, 161, 165, 168
peace 17, 21–3, 26–7, 34, 37–59, 74,
    91, 97, 135, 146, 158, 166–7, 183
Peace 911 45–6
Peace Beyond Borders (Mehta) 53–4
permaculture 63, 94–5
Permaculture Paradise Institute
    (PPI) 94–5
pessimism 42

Pew Research Centre 62
Philippines 44–5
Pillars of Positive Peace 43–4
Pinker, Steven 6, 39, 41–2, 146, 158
Playing for Change 50
poetry 8–9
Polman, Paul 63
Poppleton 5, 16, 77–9, 155
Population Health Management
    (PHM) 76
Positive Intelligence (Chamine) 143,
    148
Positive Peace 42–8
Positive Peace, Cultural Wellbeing
    and Youth Agency Initiative 47
poverty 1, 6, 21, 85, 91, 95, 168
prayer 38
Primeast 24, 26, 32–3, 57, 72, 94,
    106, 109, 120, 123–5, 143, 152,
    186, 189, 196–7
PrimeFocus™ 27, 186, 197
Purposeful Leadership 5, 8, 19,
    32, 65, 151, 163, 166, 183, 186,
    196–7

quantum physics 14

Rak, Olga 33–4
Ramos-Horta, Jose 53
rationality 6, 42, 146
*Rationality: What It Is, Why It Seems
    Scarce, Why It Matters* (Pinker) 42,
    146
religion 18
Restrepo, Federico 111–12
Resurgence Magazine 49
Rethink Food 46, 96–7
Rethinking Humanity (Arbib & Seba)
    64
RethinkX 61, 64, 67, 85, 91, 93, 147,
    158
Reykjavik 26
Riordan, Tom 96
Ro, Christine 64
Rowell, Jesse 57–8
Royal Liverpool Philharmonic
    Orchestra (RLPO) 50

Royal United Hospitals Bath National Health Service Trust 72–3
Russia 49, 54

Santiano, Irene 45
Scaling Leadership (Anderson & Adams) 125
scarcity 40, 86
Scharmer, Otto 149
Schumacher, Ernst 49, 84
scuba diver 2
Seba, Tony 64, 93
self-similarity 4, 5
Sinek, Simon 154–155
Skipton Building Society 106
Slezak, Michael 62
Smajlovic, Vedran 48
Small Is Beautiful (Schumacher) 84
solar 91, 98, 101–2
Spinelli, Altiero 23
Spirit of Humanity Forum 26–8
Standard Bank 31
St George's Crypt 51
Stills, Stephen 20
Sudan 45
Sunak, Rishi 23
supply chains 16–17, 24
Sustainable Development Goals (SDGs) 1–4, 21–2, 24–6, 34, 41–2, 45, 64, 66, 91, 96, 111–12, 117, 163–4, 184, 187, 191, 194, 197–8
Sweden 121
Swiss Green Liberal Party 33–4
Swiss National Council 34
Syria 2

Tarver, Simon 124
Tesla 63, 93
The Better Angels of our Nature–Why Violence Has Declined (Pinker) 42
The Future of Leadership is Integral Informed by Unity (Anderson) 126
Theory U (Scharmer) 149
Thompson, Alfredo 72–3

Thunberg, Greta 20–1, 147
tourism 15
Townley, Tony 100–2
Treaty of Lisbon 23
29k Foundation 163

Uganda 44–5
UK Asset Resolution Limited (UKAR) 107
Ukraine 22, 39–40, 54
United Kingdom (UK) 15–16, 22–3, 30, 49, 57, 66–7, 70, 72, 74, 84, 92, 95, 97, 101, 107, 111, 127, 186–7, 196
United Nations (UN) 1, 3, 21–3, 24–6, 34, 40, 42–3, 45, 49, 61, 64, 66, 70, 91–2, 96, 106, 111–12, 117, 157, 163, 184, 187, 191, 194, 197
United Nations Association (UNA) 1, 22, 70, 92, 94, 96
United States (US) 22, 49, 64, 85, 87, 93, 117, 153
Uniting for Peace 53
unity consciousness 14, 125–6
University of Cambridge 111
University of Central Lancashire (UCLan) 113–14
University of Oxford 7
Usher, Jen 106–7

Villapalos, Clare Leon 80
violence 39–40, 42, 55
Vision of Humanity 44
vitality 5, 40, 51, 56, 60–82, 97, 102, 125, 135, 155, 167
VUCA 126

Walker-Martin, Francesca 113–14
Walsh, Matt 8, 47, 74–7, 102–3
war 1, 6, 18, 20–3, 37–42, 45–6, 48, 54, 56–7, 110, 126, 161
Wibberley, Owen 57–8
Wilson, Frances 152
Wilson, Helen 50
Wilson, Margaret 127
Wilson, Sally 127

204 Index

Winston, Andrew 63
wisdom 4, 9, 14, 17, 25, 39, 41, 51–2, 57, 84, 87, 99, 116–29, 135, 144–5, 149, 151, 158–78, 195
Wisdom Code 4, 41, 117, 128, 159–78
woodmeadows 70–1
Woodstock 50
women 41, 45, 52, 54, 62, 162
World War II 23, 110

Worldview Dynamics and the Well-Being of Nations (Barrett) 119

YouTube 12, 48, 51, 54–5, 58, 64, 96, 102, 117, 122, 155

Zambia 56
Zen and the Art of Making a Living (Boldt) 20
Zimbabwe 56

Printed in the United States
by Baker & Taylor Publisher Services